ADVANCE PRAISE FOR *Street Wise:*
A Guide for Teen Investors
BY Janet Bamford

SELECTED BY THE TEEN PEOPLE BOOK CLUB

"When I was a teen and already interested in the market, my father told me that if I wanted to know a stock as well as anyone, I could. I feel that advice gave me an advantage over my journalistic peers. **Today, as more and more young people get involved in the exciting world of investing, there couldn't be a better time for a book like this. I wish there had been something like this for me when I was a kid**."

JONATHAN STEINBERG
Chairman and Editor in Chief
Individual Investor Group, Inc.

"Janet Bamford's book not only points out what most teens don't know about economics and financial decision making, but, more importantly, it helps them (in a readable and clear manner) to become educated savers and investors. The book addresses an extremely important topic in today's society and its lessons will help produce literate economic citizens for the new century."

WILLIAM KEMPEY
Chairman, Department of Economics and
    Finance, Kean University
President, NJ Council on Economic Education

"Teens who read *Street Wise: A Guide for Teen Investors* will realize how easy it really is to become a millionaire by starting to invest in stocks NOW!"

TODD ROMER
President and Publisher, *Young Money* magazine

"Bamford's book is **a must-read not only for Stock Market Game players, but also for my high schoolers** who all need to know financial information, including how important a Roth IRA is."

> **PAT MORRIS**
> Teacher, Whippany Park High School, New Jersey

"**How I wish I'd had a handbook like this as a teen: friendly, conversational tone, great investment information, and powerful testimonials from young people who have achieved financial success**. Parents—a great find for you as well."

> **BONITA (BONI) CALLAWAY, CMFC, EA**
> Financial Education Coordinator
> INVESCO Funds

"With all the exciting career choices for teenagers, it is critical that they also learn the basics about managing and investing their own money. **Janet Bamford has done an excellent job of reducing some very complex topics into a very understandable and practical format.**"

> **JEFFERY D. FOX, CFA**
> Director, Educational Development
> National Association of Investors Corporation
> (NAIC)

"***Street Wise* is an excellent book to help young people understand their investment options.** This book provides a good foundation of basic investment information for teens to consider as they explore their alternatives."

> **ELIZABETH SCHIEVER**
> National Endowment for Financial Education
> Director, High School Financial Planning Program

Street
Wise

Other Titles from Bloomberg Press

INVESTING 101
by Kathy Kristof

INVESTING IN IPOs: NEW PATHS TO PROFIT
WITH INITIAL PUBLIC OFFERINGS
by Tom Taulli

INVESTING IN SMALL-CAP STOCKS:
REVISED EDITION
by Christopher Graja and Elizabeth Ungar

THE NEW COMMONSENSE GUIDE TO MUTUAL FUNDS
by Mary Rowland

THE WINNING PORTFOLIO:
CHOOSING YOUR 10 BEST MUTUAL FUNDS
by Paul B. Farrell

A complete list of our titles is available at
www.Bloomberg.com/Books

BLOOMBERG PERSONAL BOOKSHELF

Street Wise

A Guide for Teen Investors

by Janet Bamford

BLOOMBERG PRESS
PRINCETON

First edition published 2000
1 3 5 7 9 10 8 6 4 2

Library of Congress Cataloging-in-Publication Data

Bamford, Janet
    Street wise: a guide for teen investors / Janet Bamford.–1st ed.
      p.   cm.
    Includes index.
    Summary: An investment guide for new investors, including stock market games and investment clubs, interviews with teens who have invested, investing advice, and additional resources.
      ISBN 1-57660-039-4
      1. Saving and investment—Juvenile literature. 2. Teenagers—Finance, Personal—Juvenile literature. [1. Saving and investment. 2. Finance, Personal.] I. Title.

HG4521 .B34524 2000
332.6–dc21   00-024724

Edited by Jared Kieling

Book design by Barbara Diez Goldenberg

For my kids, Peter, Gregory, and Julia
May you learn the true value of both time and money

Acknowledgments

IT IS COMMON TO BEMOAN THE FACT that personal finance and investing are not taught in many schools. But what I have found is that where these subjects are taught, they are often taught very well, by a cadre of teachers doing their best to make sure the next generation is ready for the world they'll face when they hit adulthood. I am grateful to the teachers and students who shared their insights and experiences with me. This group includes, but is not limited to, Mark Amantia, Jim Buchanan, Jerry Cooper, Kaye Corrigan, Beth Hamm, Chris Labeots, Patricia Matthews, Pat Morris, and Joan Morrissey.

I am also indebted to the Wall Street professionals and observers who took time to talk with me, including Jim Cramer; Andrew, Chris and Shelby Davis; Alexandra Lebenthal; John Neff; and Jonathan Steinberg. Numerous parents and young investors were happy to share their enthusiasm for investing and first-hand knowledge of how to get kids involved in it. I am also beholden to the investment club community, including Jeff Fox at the NAIC, and Grafton Daniels of St. George's Junior Investment Club, a model for how a youth investment club can work. Thanks, too, to the New Jersey Stock Market Game staff, including Bill Kempey and Steve Clark, and the national Stock Market Game and Lisa Donnini for their input.

At Bloomberg Press, my thanks go to Jared Kieling, my editor without peer, Barbara Diez, and Maris Williams for the care they lavished on this manuscript. Lynn Seligman, my agent, helped shape this book initially, and my colleagues at *Bloomberg Personal Finance* magazine, particularly Steve Gittelson and Chris Miles, were generous and perceptive with editorial assistance.

To my husband, David Coats, and my children, Peter, Gregory, and Julia, thank you for your support and patience.

Introduction

DON'T LET ANYONE TELL YOU THAT YOU'RE TOO young to understand investing. Don't get scared off, either, by all the complications that people dream up for discussing, dissecting, and analyzing the stock market. The great thing about investing is that you can start slowly, bit by bit, and get more deeply involved as you learn more. You don't need to know it all at once to get a good start. Remember, you have time. "The important thing to know about this business is that it's arithmetic," says James J. Cramer, a professional money manager and a cofounder of TheStreet.com. "My daughter's second-grade class covers virtually everything I need to know about math and the stock market."

The idea behind investing is to make your money work for you. And given half a chance, it will work very hard indeed. Over the past century, the stock market has paid higher returns to investors than banks, bonds, and any similar investments. Properly invested, over time your money will earn more than you can imagine, thanks to the miracle of compound investing, which you'll learn about in Chapter 2. You need not begin investing with large sums of money, either. The key to long-term investment success is regular investing and an early start, not a large initial grubstake.

Trading in the stock market interests almost everyone these days for a number of reasons. The percentage of Americans who own stocks is at all-time-high levels. Baby boomers, conscious that they can't depend on Uncle Sam to provide financial security for their future, are stashing chunks of their paychecks into retirement programs, and much of that money has poured into the stock market. Young adults have turned to the market in large numbers, too. A study by the National Association of Securities Dealers (NASD) showed that Gen X investors (defined as eighteen to thirty-four years old) make up 19 percent of investors and that a large percentage participate in automatic withdrawal investment programs. All of these groups add to the flow of money into the market, helping to keep it strong.

In addition, online trading has made it possible to buy and sell stocks less expensively and more easily than ever before. So more and more people see the stock market as a normal part of their daily concerns. This book will explain the ways you can get involved in trading—and making money—now, even before you're old enough to vote.

THE CHAPTERS COVER the following topics:
>>How to establish a custodial account, which you'll need until you're twenty-one
>>The nuts and bolts of investing
>>Whether to use a full-service or discount broker
>>Understanding online investing

>>How to handle a stock market nosedive
>>Tax concerns
>>How big-name investors got started
>>Investment clubs and games
>>Finding resources on the Internet
>>Wall Street careers you might want to consider someday

YOU'LL DISCOVER that many teens are actively involved in the stock market already. You can join them—just turn the page.

"Dollars do better
if they are
accompanied
by sense."

EARL RINEY, CLERGYMAN

1

What's in This for You

WHEN IT COMES TO MAKING MONEY BY INVESTING, time is on your side. Start early.

You probably know something about the stock market. If you watch the news on television, you can't miss the daily reports of what happened on Wall Street. You may have seen business magazines around the house, or your parents may talk about stocks at the dinner table.

You might even have stocks or mutual funds held in custodial accounts for you. A surprising number of kids do. While no regulatory agency tracks the number of custodial accounts, Merrill Lynch commissioned a survey on kids and money and asked the survey firm to estimate the number of kids between the ages of twelve and seventeen who have stocks or mutual funds held for them in custodial accounts. (See "Money Survey," pages 14–15.) An estimated 2.3 million twelve-to-seventeen-year-olds own mutual funds, while approximately 2.5 million own stocks.

What you may not realize is how investing and the stock market will play a vital role in your future, no matter what you choose to do with your life. Whether you want to build a career in business, be a freelance artist, or become an Internet million-aire, knowing about managing your own money will give you freedom and choices in life that you wouldn't otherwise have.

STREET SMARTS<

If you had invested **$1,000** in **Microsoft** when it went public in March 1986, your stock would be worth **$473,760** today.

The truth is that you are going to need to know more about investing than your par-ents or your grandparents ever had to know. For better or worse, over the past several years there has been a trend toward ordinary people handling their own money rather than depending on an institution to do it for them. "I'm thirty-one now, and I have been investing since the middle of high school," says Todd Romer, publisher of *Young Money*, a financial magazine for teens. "I was always amazed that all my peers weren't doing this. Individuals have to take the bull by the horns—take responsibility and get control of their money."

In the old days, it was standard for people to work for a sin-gle company for most of their careers and retire to collect a guaranteed pension. That's still the model for some people, but it's far more likely that over the course of your life, you'll change jobs several times—and perhaps even change careers. Not many employers offer a pension with guaranteed benefits these days; instead they have retirement plans that both employer and employee may contribute to. In fact, one of the early decisions you will have to make when you finish your education and start working full time is how you want your 401(k) money invested. (A 401(k) is a retirement savings plan that workers, and often their employers, contribute to. A worker decides among the choices offered by the employer's plan how that money should be invested.) That's just one reason you'll need to know about investments.

There are other reasons. Even if someday you choose to have a professional money manager handle your affairs the way a teenage movie star does, you need to know what's going on, or you risk being taken advantage of. "I learned about investing not because anyone thought I was going to go into it as a career," says Chris Davis, a mutual funds manager who started learning about investing as a kid. "My father felt strongly that you had to spend some time to learn how to manage your own money. There are a lot of charlatans in the business, but it wasn't difficult to learn what you need to know to recognize if you're being taken advantage of. You need to learn how to make sense of the idiocy that is served up as general financial planning advice by some. Whether you become a doctor or a priest or whatever, learning how to manage your money is an important part of your education."

> STREET SMARTS

Average number of shares traded every day on the New York Stock Exchange:
• in 1988: **161 million**
• in 1999: **674 million**

Studies show that the average teen in America doesn't know a lot about investing. In a survey done by the Jump$tart Coalition for Financial Literacy, a group that promotes financial education, only 14.4 percent of 1,500 high school seniors polled understood that stocks would probably have a higher return than a savings account, a checking account, or a U.S. savings bond over the next eighteen years. (Of course, studies also show that the average adult doesn't know a lot more.)

But just as it has never been so important for teens to know about investing, it has never been so easy to learn and to get started. Commissions and fees on stocks and funds are falling, and a wealth of information is available to the average investor.

One of the mistakes that many kids—as well as adults— make is thinking that the stock market is too complicated and that only professionals can master it. Andrew Hamm, now a student at the University of Michigan, started investing when he was in high school. "I think the biggest misconception kids have is that a normal person can't invest," he says. "You don't have to have a master's in business to have the skills to invest." If you can understand simple mathematics, including addition, subtraction, and percentages, you know enough to learn the basics of investing.

Another pitfall of would-be investors is thinking of investing as being like spinach: good for you, but not something you're dying to try.

Investing *is* good for you, but it can also be endlessly fascinating. "I do this because it's fun," says Dan Abrahamson, a Connecticut high school student. "When I was ten years old, my big passions were baseball cards and comic books. My grandfather convinced me that I should buy stock in Marvel Comics. I bought it at 20, and it went to 56, split two for one, and then I sold it at 31. It tripled in about a year's time. I was hooked. I started watching CNBC. My grandfather and I would call each other with tips. We'd talk every day." (See Chapter 3, page 50, for an explanation of stock splits.)

STREET SMARTS<

When *American Heritage* magazine ranked the richest Americans of all time, the top five were **John D. Rockefeller, Andrew Carnegie, Cornelius Vanderbilt, John Jacob Astor,** and **William H. Gates III.**

Some kids have their interest kindled more slowly. "My grandfather used to give me ten shares of stock for Christmas, and I'd think, 'You've got to be kidding,'" says Kirsten Hagen, a student at DePauw University in Illinois. "I didn't appreciate it. But I started following the market in high school and did some trading, and when I turned eighteen I took over my portfolio and began to teach myself different ways to research stocks." Hagen was a cofounder of her college investment club, something we'll talk about in Chapter 8.

Investing is exciting. Stock prices change throughout every trading day, in response to world events (a plane crash or a hurricane can affect dozens of stocks: those of the companies involved, their insurance companies, and their suppliers); corporate competition; or even the season. Teens are finding great stock ideas by looking at the products they and their friends are enthusiastic about, and we'll see how they are turning that knowledge into profits for themselves.

Ah, yes: money. Investing is about making money with the money you have. And while the young investors we've talked to have been interested in long-term strategies and haven't cashed in their stocks and left the market, make no mistake: there's no age minimum for making a profit from investing.

> **STREET SMARTS**

47% of stock owners are female; 53% are male.

Jay Liebowitz, a Californian who started the Web site Wall Street Wizard (see Chapter 10, page 189) and is now a University of Pennsylvania student, started investing at thirteen and quadrupled his money picking stocks like Cisco and Microsoft. Jason Orlovsky is another example. The eighteen-year-old New Jersey high school senior started investing after he received about $5,000 for his bar mitzvah. Over the next five years, he made some uncommonly shrewd investments, most notably as an early investor in a company called CMGI, which owns stakes in Internet companies. His shares in CMGI, which he bought at about $3.50 a share, were worth about $281 a share at the time of this writing. Over the past five years he's pumped about $5,000 of savings into his portfolio, and his investments were recently worth some $342,000. Anticipating college expenses next year, Jason has moved about $80,000 of his portfolio into more conservative mutual funds but is keeping the bulk of the technology stocks that he's done so well with. Although the poised Eagle Scout (his other passions, besides the stock market, include camping and rock climbing) has exercised

The Power of Compounding

YOU ARE THE ENVY OF YOUR ELDERS. Adults may have a bigger cash cash cushion on their side when they invest, but you have an advantage they've lost and will never have again: time.

The magic of compound interest depends on time to work, and that's what you have plenty of. Compounding has been called "the eighth wonder of the world." I would rank it higher than that. To see how it works, let's use the example of money in a savings account.

In a savings account, your money earns interest, which is added to your account total. Then that higher total earns more interest. At its most basic, compounding means that the interest also earns interest.

Given enough time, compound interest adds up in ways that amaze.

Here's an example: if someone offered to give you either $1,000 a day for a month or a penny that doubled in value every day for a month, which would you choose? If you understand the power of compound interest, you'd take the penny. After thirty days of daily doubling, that penny would be worth $5.4 million. Look at the table at right to see how it adds up!

admirable restraint in not spending his investment gains, he did take enough cash out of his portfolio to buy his mother's used Ford Explorer for $17,000 last year, after he got his driver's license. That's a dividend any teen can appreciate. (See "The Power of Compounding," above.)

A more realistic example is equally powerful. Had you invested $10,000 in the Standard and Poor's 500 stock index in 1978 and reinvested all dividends, twenty years later your shares would have been worth $244,279.

DAY	TOTAL $	DAY	TOTAL $
1	.01	16	327.68
2	.02	17	655.36
3	.04	18	1,310.72
4	.08	19	2,621.44
5	.16	20	5,242.88
6	.32	21	10,485.76
7	.64	22	20,971.52
8	1.28	23	41,943.04
9	2.56	24	83,886.08
10	5.12	25	167,772.16
11	10.24	26	335,544.32
12	20.48	27	671,088.64
13	40.96	28	1,342,177.28
14	81.92	29	2,684,354.56
15	163.84	30	5,368,709.12

So the reason that your youth is such an advantage is that you have decades of investing ahead of you. And while the stock market is famous for going up and going down, over any thirty-year time span since its creation, you never would have lost money in the market, including during the period that encompasses the Great Depression.

The lesson here? Get money in the market when you're young, leave it there, and add to it regularly. (See "How Long Until My Money Doubles? The Rule of 72," page 12.)

How Long Until My Money Doubles?
The Rule of 72

FOR GENERATIONS, STUDENTS of all ages have had one big question for their teachers: Will this be on the test?

If there were such a thing as the test of life, the Rule of 72 would definitely be on it. Memorize it, because you will use it, I promise. It also has the great virtue of being easy to remember and use.

The Rule of 72 is very straightforward. To find out how long it will take your money to double, divide the number 72 by the rate of return you expect to get. The answer will equal the number of years it will take your money to double at that rate.

Let's do the math. If you are earning a 10 percent rate of return on your money, divide 72 by 10 to equal 7.2. (72/10=7.2) It will take 7.2 years for your money to double. Getting an 8 percent return? 72/8=9. It will take 9 years for your money to double. Getting 5 percent? 72/5=14.4. At 5 percent, you're looking at 14.4 years before it doubles.

This is the kind of equation you should be carrying around in your brain's toolbox. Haul it out whenever you need to make some quick calculations about investment returns.

Ten years from now, if someone tries to sell you on a product by saying you can double your money in three years, you'll be able to quickly figure that they are promising you an impossible-to-guarantee 24 percent a year. You'll know better than to fall for that.

TEENS AND WALL STREET

HAVE YOU SEEN THE TV ADS FOR CHARLES SCHWAB, THE DIS-count and online brokerage firm? One recent ad shows eighteen-year-old Russian tennis star Anna Kournikova talking with competitors not about tennis strategy or athletic endorsements but about price-earnings ratios and mutual funds. The message is clear: even a young, busy, world-ranked athlete has the time and the brains to learn about investing. Schwab, like lots of companies, has taken notice of your generation.

Everyone has heard of the baby boomers—your parents' generation, which was born in the fifteen or so years after World War II and has had a huge impact on the economy and popular culture. But the current teenage population—often called "Generation Y" or "Generation Next"—is bigger than the baby boom generation. There are now about 39.6 million kids between the ages of ten and nineteen, according to the Census Bureau, and that number will climb to 41.6 million by 2005.

That growth hasn't escaped Wall Street, which is looking for ways to teach kids about investing in the hope that they'll become longtime customers. Several firms have started mutual fund programs aimed at young investors, such as American Express, Stein Roe, and USAA. Stein Roe started its Young Investor Fund in 1994, after the firm's survey of junior high school kids showed that they were interested in learning about money and personal finance but had no formal channels to do so. The fund now has 200,000 investors and $1 billion in assets under management. Some 70 percent of the accounts are custodial accounts,

> **>YOUNG INVESTOR POLL**
> Who would you rather be like:
> Michael Jordan or Bill Gates?
> •29% said Bill Gates.
> •21% said Michael Jordan.
> •**50% said they'd rather be themselves.**
> SOURCE: BUCKINVESTOR.COM

13 < <

Money Survey

MERRILL LYNCH, the big brokerage firm, commissioned a telephone survey of kids between the ages of twelve and seventeen in February 2000. Below are some excerpts from the survey results. The survey was conducted by International Communications Research (ICR), a research firm that questions teens about different issues, as part of its TeenEXCEL project. While ICR obviously didn't talk to every teen in America, it designed its research taking into account variations in the teen population. The result is that the answers are "projectable to the whole population"—in other words, they fairly represent the whole population of U.S. kids ages twelve to seventeen. It's fun to see how you measure up against your peers.

One note: for the different categories below, keep in mind that multiple answers were accepted, so the percentages may add up to more than 100 percent. (For instance, a teen might have responded that she gets money both from her parents and from doing odd jobs around the house.)

>>**Where do you get money?**
83% get money from their parents when they need it.
72% earn money by doing odd jobs.
38% have a regular allowance.
22% have regular jobs (older teens are more likely to have such jobs).

>>**What kind of financial accounts do you have?**
Of all twelve-to-seventeen-year-olds:
65% have a savings account.

22% have a checking account.

12% own mutual funds.

12% own stocks.

>> **Have any of your classes in school ever discussed saving money or investing?**
- •Male   55% yes
          45% no
- •Female   50% yes
            50% no

>> **What do you do with your money?**

59% usually spend half and save half of the money they get.

24% save most of it.

17% spend most of it immediately.

>> **How much do you earn at your job?**

The median wage they earn is $5.70 an hour.

The median number of hours they work is 15 hours a week.

>> **What do you save for?**

42% are saving for college.

30% are saving to buy a car.

18% are not saving for anything in particular or don't know.

8% are saving for a specific item.

7% are saving to buy clothes.

2% are saving to pay car expenses.

SOURCE: MERRILL, LYNCH, PIERCE, FENNER & SMITH INC. REPRINTED WITH PERMISSION.

with an average balance of $4,106; the average shareholder is about twelve years old.

Salomon Smith Barney started its Young Investors Network in 1997; the project's Web site has about 12,000 registered users. Salomon Smith Barney also started a pilot program of three-day in-school investing workshops in selected schools and is trying out a summer workshop on investing for girls. Since the Young Investors Network started, the company has seen a 22 percent increase in custodial accounts, although, says Mindy Ross, Salomon Smith Barney senior vice president, other factors could have contributed to that.

STREET SLANG<

BULL MARKET

A market where most **stocks are rising.** Easy to remember if you picture a bull tossing its horns up. **Wall Street loves bulls,** which is why you constantly see them in brokerage firm ads.

But the business world isn't interested solely in the business you'll do with them someday—they're looking at the considerable economic power you wield right now. Think you don't have money to put into the stock market? Think again. Teens spent about $153 billion in 1999, according to Teenage Research Unlimited, a market research firm. In 1999, the newspaper *USA Today* called you "The Richest Generation of Teens," finding that nearly half of the kids surveyed had spent at least $20 in stores within the last week. Since most teens don't have to pay for things like housing, groceries, and electricity, as their parents do and as they will once they're living on their own, their income is largely "discretionary."

So now is the perfect time to get started investing—even with small amounts of money.

"I was working with
elementary school kids
in a class on the stock
market and one boy wrote
to a cereal company
for information. They
sent him a coloring book,
and his reaction was,
'what do they think I am,
some little kid?
I wanted to see
an annual report.'"

MICHIGAN TEACHER

Stock Market 101

IF YOU'RE JUST GETTING ACQUAINTED WITH INVEST-ing and the stock market, the first thing you need to know is that the ideas behind investing are really very basic. This isn't rocket science, guys. Anyone who can understand the concept of offsides in a soccer game—as can millions of American kids—is more than qualified to master the basics of investing.

As we've said before, you don't need to know everything before you start tucking away some money. When you're a teenager, the biggest enemy of successful investing is inertia—the tendency to do nothing. The best way to combat that tendency is to take a few steps toward learning about investing, then take a few steps in actually doing it. These can be the most profitable steps you've ever taken.

SAVING AND INVESTING

IF YOU'RE READING THIS, YOU PROBABLY ALREADY KNOW something about saving money. Before you—or anyone—can invest, you need to have extra money. At first glance, "extra money" sounds like two words that don't belong next to each other. To many of your contemporaries, the way to handle money is to spend it. If you have $5, you spend $5; if you have $100, go ahead and spend $100.

But as you know, that's no way to live. There are few things more pathetic than someone who has never learned to live beneath his or her means (not just within it!). Long-term goals—like buying a car, helping pay for college, or even, later in life, owning a home—are out of your reach if you don't get in the habit of spending less than you make.

STREET SMARTS<

Wall Street got its name because early settlers of Manhattan built a stockade fence—**a wall**—at the town's northern boundary. A street was laid alongside the wall in 1685. The wall was taken down as the city grew northward.

As a kid, you acquire money in a few different ways. Parents and grandparents might give you some money, in the form of allowance and gifts. And there are plenty of opportunities to earn money, whether through occasional jobs, like baby-sitting, lawn mowing, or snow shoveling, or through regular jobs, like working in a store or restaurant.

You have different things to spend money on, too. Like going to movies, going on dates, eating out with friends, and buying clothes and CDs. Enjoy. But before you spend all the money that comes into your possession, get in the habit of putting some aside. If you were to learn and adopt only one lesson from this entire book, I would hope it would be this one: as soon as possible, start saving 10 percent of your income. If your income is $10 a month, save $1; if it's $100 a month, save $10. I realize that saving $1 a month may sound a little ridiculous. But you are establishing an important habit. That 10 percent is low enough that you ought to be able to get along without it yet high enough to really add up over time. Stash it away before you are even tempted to spend it.

Stash it where? What do you do with your savings? The first place any kid should learn to save money is in a savings account at your local bank. (It will at least get the money out of your sock drawer, where you might be tempted to spend it.) The bank will pay you interest, and your money will begin to add up. But once you've saved a moderate amount in a savings account—perhaps a couple hundred dollars—you should think about other places for your money. The interest rates that banks will pay on a savings account are pretty low right now, and if you're going to put your money to work, it might as well work hard.

So what else can you do with your money to make sure it will earn more money for you? Invest it in the stock market. As you can see by the table on the following page, from 1926 to 1999, stocks have paid higher returns to investors than other types of investments, such as bonds.

WHAT IS A STOCK?

OWNING A SHARE OF STOCK MEANS THAT YOU OWN PART OF A company. It is rather comforting to think of stocks this way. Buying a share of Microsoft means that you and Bill Gates are business partners. (Sort of. Don't expect an invitation to his house to meet the family anytime soon!)

Companies sell **stock** (sometimes referred to as **equity**) primarily to pay for the costs of starting or expanding their business. For example, let's say you decide to start a company, Sole Survivor, to manufacture a new line of athletic shoes. You think

Which Investments Have the Highest Return?

WE DON'T HAVE A CRYSTAL BALL to predict the future, but looking at the long-term past performance of different assets (types of investments) can provide the best clue to where you should invest your money. Below you can see how different investments performed in the seventy-four years from 1926 through 1999. This table shows how, even with the ups and downs of the market, stocks have provided a higher return than other investments. Bonds (which are like loans investors make to companies and governments) of all types and Treasury bills (which are like very short term bonds) haven't provided a return even half as high as stocks.

ASSET	AVERAGE ANNUAL RETURN
Large-company stocks (S&P 500 Index)	11.3%
Corporate bonds	5.6%
Long-term government bonds	4.8%
U.S. Treasury bills	3.7%
Inflation	3.1%

SOURCE: WIESENBERGER, THOMSON FINANCIAL

the cutting-edge design you've come up with will attract zillions of buyers. You can just imagine the profits rolling in now.

But you're going to need some money to start this company. You need to buy manufacturing equipment, pay the salaries of your workers, buy raw materials, rent a factory and an office, pay for advertising—there are all sorts of expenses involved in launching and running a business.

How Much Would a Dollar Have Grown?

WHAT DO THE NUMBERS in the table at left mean? To get a good sense of how an 11.3 percent or 5.6 percent compound annual growth rate can add up, look at the table below. It shows how much a dollar would have grown over 70-plus years in different investments. In order to calculate these numbers, Wiesenberger, Thomson Financial assumed that there were no taxes or transaction costs, and assumed all dividends would be reinvested. So your real life results would have been different than the numbers here. However, the table still gives you a sense of how much higher the return on stocks has been than on other investments.

IF YOU INVESTED $1 AT THE END OF 1925 IN:	IN 1999, YOUR INVESTMENT WOULD HAVE BEEN WORTH:
Large company stocks (S&P 500 Index)	$2,821.53
Corporate bonds	$57.45
Long-term government bonds	$31.66
U.S. Treasury bills	$14.80
Inflation rate: what $1 would be worth in 1999	$9.41

SOURCE: WIESENBERGER, THOMSON FINANCIAL

Where is this money going to come from? When you start a company, the money may at first come from your own savings, or perhaps from friends and family who decide to chip in. You can also borrow money from banks. But another way is to sell parts of the company—shares of stock—to people. They give you money, you give them a tiny piece of the company. When you sell stock, you are promising to give a bit of the company's profits to the other owners, or stockholders.

When a company is just starting up, often business owners will sell part of it to a small group of venture capitalists—professional investors who buy into new companies that they think are promising. Venture capitalists are hoping to find the next Home Depot or Yahoo!, help finance its growth, and prosper in that way.

So now Sole Survivor has several different owners. You own some of the stock (probably the largest chunk), the venture capitalists own some, and let's just bet that your mother bought into the firm, too. Perhaps you've decided there will be 100,000 shares of stock in all. If you own 50,001 shares, you have a controlling interest, because you own more than half of the company. (Companies, like democracies, are generally ruled on a one-share, one-vote basis. In very large companies, however, you can effectively wield control of the firm while owning less than 50 percent.) Your venture capitalist buddies may own 40 percent, or 40,000 shares, and your mom might have bought 9,999 shares. If I came along and bought one share, I'd own $\frac{1}{100,000}$ of the company. My $\frac{1}{100,000}$ is not a big piece, but I still own part of the company. (Microsoft, for example, has about 5 billion outstanding shares and approximately 3 million shareholders, which gives you a clue why you haven't been asked over to the Gates's for dinner.)

Anyway, Sole Survivor prospers. The year ends, and the company has made a nice profit. The company's management (you)

> **STREET SLANG<**
> ―――――――――――――
> **PREFERRED STOCK**
> Preferred by whom? This kind of stock has a **fixed dividend** that neither rises nor falls— even if the company increases the dividend for the common stockholders. Preferred stock also usually can be **"called"** by a company, which means you're **required to sell it back.** The drawback is that it can sometimes be called at prices below the market price.

might decide to put some of that profit back into the company—to buy newer, bigger manufacturing equipment. But you may also decide to declare a dividend, and pay some of the profit to the stockholders. Since you own roughly half of the company, you get roughly half of whatever profits you decide to hand out; my take is limited to my $1/100,000$th.

Earning dividends is one way to make money as a stockholder. The other—and this is where the real money comes in—is owning stock whose price goes up.

Let's go back for a minute to Sole Survivor. So far, the company as I've described it is private—the stock is owned by only a few people, and it isn't sold on a stock exchange. At some point, with Sole Survivor doing well, you want to expand further. Business looks good; America

> STREET SLANG

BIG BOARD
The New York Stock Exchange.

can't get enough of your shoes, and you want to build more factories and also try to sell your shoes overseas. It takes big money to do this. You decide to raise more money by "going public"—selling stock to the public on the stock exchanges in what's called an initial public offering, or an IPO. Typically, some of the early private investors—perhaps the founders, the venture capitalists, or even mom—will decide to cash in and sell some of their shares in an IPO. The rest of the proceeds from the IPO go to the company. (Of course, as you can imagine, lawyers and investment bankers help steer the company through this "going public" process, and they are paid handsomely.) Once a company goes public, anyone can buy and sell shares of it on a stock exchange, and the price of the stock is determined by that public trading.

The companies that you can buy stock in are the publicly owned companies traded on stock exchanges like the New York Stock Exchange, the American Stock Exchange, and Nasdaq (the American Stock Exchange has now merged with Nasdaq).

Quiz: Public or Private?

WHAT'S THE DIFFERENCE between public companies and private companies? Both make and sell things for the general public, can be large or small, and can be involved in any industry they wish. The difference is that you and I can buy stock in public firms but not in private ones. Sometimes private firms are family owned, and sometimes they're principally owned by employees and executives.

Can you guess which of the following companies are publicly held and which are privately held? (See below for the answers.)

Borden	Snacks, pasta
Del Monte Foods	Canned vegetables and fruits
Fidelity Investments	Mutual funds, financial services
Hallmark	Greeting cards
J Crew	Clothing
Levi Strauss	Jeans, Dockers
L.L. Bean	Clothing and sporting goods
Mars	Candy

STUMPED? All of the firms listed above are privately held. For the investors who would dearly love to own stock in them, take heart. Private companies often go public, allowing them to expand and allowing the private stockholders to cash out some of their holdings. It was only in 1999, for instance, that UPS, the package delivery company known for its brown trucks, and Goldman Sachs, the well-known securities and investment banking firm, converted their status from private to public company.

Take a look at the quiz at left. Can you guess which of the companies listed are public and which are private?

One big change for companies that go public is that they are required to meet all kinds of regulations they didn't have to meet as private companies. For example, they must begin reporting financial results to the public. Public companies have to put out an annual report to tell investors how well they've done in the past year, and they are regulated by the Securities and Exchange Commission (SEC), which is the main government agency overseeing the financial markets. It is the SEC that punishes companies if they release false or misleading financial information to investors. This is designed to give investors a more level playing field (the Wall Street pros and the company's own executives aren't supposed to be able to profit from information that isn't available to the public) and to promote confidence in the stock markets. It has worked. The U.S. financial markets are the strongest in the world, in part because of securities laws.

But the SEC can't protect people against the risk that the stocks they buy will decline in price. Unlike with a bank account, there are no guarantees with stocks. If Sole Survivor loses its edge and goes out of business, your stock may be worthless—and no one will reimburse you for what you've lost. That risk—that you will lose your money—comes with the higher historic returns in the stock market. And it's important for beginners to note that not all stocks have the same degree of risk. Exxon is a more stable company, and therefore a more stable stock, than the Internet start-up of the day.

Aside from their historically high returns, one of the other big advantages of stocks as an investment is their liquidity: they're easy to sell and buy quickly. If you decide to invest your money in real estate, antiques, or Beanie Babies, you may see appreciation (a price rise on what you own), but if you want to sell out and get your money quickly, it can be hard to find a buyer.

The Reinvesting Rap

THERE IS AN OLD SAYING about real estate that can make you sound wise beyond your years: "What are the three things you need to know about buying real estate? Location, location, location." That means that you can overcome a lot of problems with a house or property, but the one thing you can't change is its location, so a good location is of the utmost importance.

A similar slogan applies to investing. What are the three things you need to know? Reinvest, reinvest, reinvest.

That means when a stock you own declares a dividend, specify that it is to be reinvested—in other words, used to buy more stock (or, more likely, fractional shares of stock, which companies allow if you are enrolled in a dividend reinvestment plan). The same goes for mutual funds, which also declare dividends.

Reinvesting the dividends makes an enormous difference over time. Had you invested $1,000 in the Standard and Poor's 500 stock index in 1978 and reinvested all dividends, twenty years later your shares would have been worth $24,428. If you had not reinvested the dividends, your shares would have been worth $15,000. That's quite a difference.

Not all companies have dividend reinvestment plans, or DRIPs, although their popularity continues to grow. To see whether a stock you're interested in has a DRIP, check out this great Web site: **www.dripcentral.com.**

Stocks can be bought and sold readily most days of the year, and you can find out how much your holdings are worth simply by checking the financial pages of the newspaper or by tapping into the Internet.

BE A LONG-TERM INVESTOR

STOCK MARKET COMMENTATORS ALWAYS TALK ABOUT BULLS and bears, but just once I'd like to hear them speak of tortoises and hares. Hares jump into the market and jump out, missing the long-term gains. The tortoise, not the bull, would be my pick for stock market emblem: slow and steady. If you'll remember your Aesop's Fables, the tortoise won. I'll take boring and profitable any day.

Promise yourself that you will be a long-term stock market investor. History shows that the superior returns in the stock market come over a period of years; the market and the economy can be down in any given year or couple of years. A superb way to stick with it is to commit to investing a specific sum of money on a regular basis, such as deciding to invest $50 a month.

My other piece of advice for long-term investors is to reinvest your earnings in the market. (See "The Reinvesting Rap," at left.)

WHAT MAKES STOCKS
GO UP AND DOWN?

COUNTLESS BOOKS, DOCTORAL THESES, AND CAREERS HAVE been devoted to asking and answering that question. The truth is that many factors affect stock prices. Like any product, how much your shares are worth is a function of whether other investors want to buy the same stock—if there is a lot of demand for your stock, the stock price will rise. The big question then becomes this: what affects demand?

Probably the largest factor is what investors think of a company's business prospects. Is the company doing well in its industry? Does it make a good product? Is the firm gaining sales (and thus seeing its revenues rise) or losing them? Does the management know how to run the firm efficiently? Is the company making profits? Does its product have a bright future (think of buggy whips versus computer technology)? Does the company have competitors that are about to eat them for lunch?

How well the economy is doing is another factor. Is the economy in the area where the company does business doing well? Is the company in a position to be taken over or to take over another company—either of which can boost a firm's stock price?

STREET SMARTS<
The **first corporate stock** traded in New York City was the **Bank of New York,** in **1791.** It's still traded today, although it has not been continuously listed.

Another factor that affects stock prices is interest rates. Turn on the evening news on any given night and you'll hear some breathless reporting about the Federal Reserve and its current chairman, Alan Greenspan, who can raise or lower the prevailing interest rates. These interest rate changes can translate into lower or higher stock prices. Think about it: if you could get a very high interest rate on money you had sitting in your guaranteed savings account at the bank, wouldn't you? So in times of high interest rates, fewer people want to buy stock in Sole Survivor. That translates into lower stock prices for the company.

'DON'T PUT ALL YOUR EGGS' AND OTHER BASIC PRINCIPLES

YOU MAY REMEMBER THE OLD SAYING "DON'T PUT ALL YOUR eggs in one basket." That is the perfect description of why you need to diversify your investments. Diversifying involves spreading your eggs around in different baskets. Even the most carefully chosen, best-researched investment should never be your only investment. At any given time there are industries whose stocks aren't doing well. If all of your money is invested in, say, Ford Motor Company, and the auto industry is having a bad year, your entire investment portfolio will be losing money. Better to own stocks in several industries and several different types of companies—small, start-up-type firms as well as large, established companies. A good rule of thumb is to own ten or twenty different stocks to achieve diversification. You don't need to buy ten stocks on the first day you begin investing, but diversification should be a goal you work toward.

>STREET SLANG

UPTICK

Has nothing to do with Lyme disease or canine parasites. An uptick is **a stock trade at a higher price than the previous trade.** Guess what a "down tick" is.

Taking the idea of diversification further, if you look at your whole portfolio, you need different categories of investments. If stocks in U.S. companies are down, perhaps international stocks will be up. When the entire stock market is down, bonds may be up.

THE RISK-REWARD RELATIONSHIP

THERE IS A LAW OF INVESTING THAT IS AS FUNDAMENTAL AND timeless as the law of gravity: risk and reward are related. The higher the potential return on an investment, the higher the risk. This is important to remember if anyone ever tries to tell you that a certain investment—a stock, a bond, or other type of investment—will earn you a lot of money. Big returns don't come without big risks.

As I've mentioned before, the biggest advantage to being an investor under the age of twenty-one is that you can afford to take more risks than older people. You have time to make up for any losses you may suffer.

Compare yourself to a sixty-year-old. That person may be only a few years away from retirement, when he or she won't be earning an income anymore and will have to live off a pension, Social Security payments, and savings. Sixty-year-olds need to be much more careful to choose investments that are less likely to lose money. You, on the other hand, have years of earning potential ahead of you.

Savings accounts, U.S. savings bonds (the kind you may have received from your grandparents), and money market accounts are all low-risk investments. They also give you lower returns.

Different stocks have different levels of risk. The typical blue-chip stocks are considered moderately risky. Initial public offerings and companies that have had financial difficulty would be considered higher risk. The real high-risk stuff is considered speculative, and speculating should be done only with money you're prepared to lose.

Asset allocation is a term you'll hear frequently over your lifetime. It refers to how money is divided up between different types of investments. One investor's asset allocation might be structured so that 80 percent of the money is in stocks, 15 percent is in bonds, and 5 percent is in a money market account.

How should a teenager allocate investment funds? Again, look at your time horizon. If you're seventeen and don't really expect to need the money any time soon (certainly not within the next five years), you are in a good position to take some risks. But if you need your money to pay for college within the next two or three years, think about shifting it to a lower-risk investment, such as a conservative mutual fund.

How much risk you should take when you invest depends not only on how old you are but also on your individual personality. Some people lie awake nights worrying about the possibility of losing their money; others thrive on taking risks in order to do better over time. The idea, of course, is to go for the maximum gain while doing everything you can to minimize risk.

And the way to do that in the stock market is to know how to research and choose an investment.

BY THE WAY, WHAT IS A BOND?

A FEW WORDS IN THE ENGLISH LANGUAGE ARE OFTEN LINKED together in a single phrase. "Peanut butter and jelly" is one of those pairings. "Stocks and bonds" is another. When you hear one of the words, it is often hitched to the other. But what exactly is a bond?

Buying a bond means you have loaned money to an entity—either a corporation or a government or government agency. Basically, a bond is an IOU from the borrower, who agrees to pay you back the money you lent at some future date, along with interest payments. You can hold a bond until maturity, which is the date when whoever borrowed the money has to pay it back, or you can sell your bond to some other investor before it matures.

Stock prices go up and down depending on investors' guesses about the future profits of the company that issued it, as well as the other factors we have discussed. Bonds change in price in the market when interest rates change. If you bought and were holding a bond that paid 5 percent interest (bonds are usually issued at current interest rates), and if interest rates went up so that new bonds were paying 6 percent, the 5 percent rate your bond would bring wouldn't be very attractive. So the price your 5 percent bond would trade for would go down. A bond's credit rating is also crucial to the value of the bond. A **credit rating** is a score published by a rating company that tells investors what the chances are that the bond's issuer—the corporation or the government organization that wants to borrow money—will be able to pay back the loan. A company with an excellent chance of repaying a bond will get an excellent

> **>STREET SMARTS**
> The **trading floor** of the New York Stock Exchange is about the size of **a football field.**

33 < <

credit rating—AAA, perhaps—while the worst credit ratings are Cs and Ds. Companies and government agencies that have bad credit ratings have to pay higher interest rates on their bonds to attract buyers; they pay more to compensate buyers for the risk they are taking in buying the bond.

Bonds are usually considered a less risky kind of investment than stocks; even if a company goes bankrupt, bondholders get paid before stockholders do. Because of their reduced risk, bonds are usually recommended as an investment for money that you can't afford to lose. As you get much older and closer to retirement, it's usually a good idea to move part of your investments into bonds. But teenagers—with an investment horizon of several decades—should look first to the stock market for investing.

SAVINGS BONDS

YOU PROBABLY HAVE A SAVINGS BOND OR TWO STASHED AWAY somewhere for safekeeping—perhaps in a parent's safe deposit box. Savings bonds are a favorite gift of grandparents and other adults.

Why are they so popular as presents? As any grandparent knows, savings bonds last longer than giving you the same amount of cash. Cash has a tendency to go through your hands, and everyone else's, too quickly. Another attraction to savings bonds is that they're easy to buy and give. You can purchase them at any bank or **credit union** (a bank-like organization run by employee groups or unions), and unlike stocks, there are no sales commissions to pay. They're as low risk an investment as was ever invented. It is unimaginable that the United States government would default on its bonds, that is, fail to pay them back. And here's a tidbit you may not know: Series EE bonds—the most common type sold—are sold at a discount to the face value. A bond with a face value of $50 costs $25. So the givers get to look a little more generous than they've actually been!

But as simple as savings bonds are, they can be a little confusing. Since this is an investment that you may well already own, here are a couple of points you will want to know about them.

Like any bond, a savings bond is a loan—in this case to the United States government.

There are different series of bonds. I'm only going to talk about Series EE bonds, since they're the most widespread. For information on the other types of bonds, go to the government's really useful Web site, **www.savingsbonds.gov**.

Series EE bonds are bought at a 50 percent reduction to their face value. If you were to cash in a $50 bond immediately after receiving it, you wouldn't get $50, because the bond wouldn't have reached maturity yet. The length of time it takes to reach maturity, when it could be cashed in for at least its face value, varies depending on when it was issued. Effective May 1, 1995, bonds are guaranteed to be worth at least face value in seventeen years, although some earlier bonds reach maturity sooner, since they were issued in a time of higher interest rates.

>STREET SLANG

BLUE CHIP

Informal term for the **stocks** of the **largest, most established companies,** which, of course, change over time. Little start-up companies can grow up to be big blue chips.

What kind of return do savings bonds earn? In the interest of allowing you to finish reading this before you sprout your first gray hair, I'll just say this: over the decades, the Treasury has fiddled with how to pay interest on savings bonds. Fiddled a lot. Consequently, the interest rate any particular bond earns depends on when it was bought. Some bonds earn whichever is

Credit Cards: The Negative Investments

IF I TOLD YOU I KNEW A WAY to earn a surefire, risk-free 18 per-cent on your money, what would you say? If you've been paying attention so far, you'd wonder what scam I was trying to sell you. That kind of return usually doesn't come risk free.

Unless it involves staying away from piling up debt on con-sumer credit cards. The interest charged on these cards can be 18 or 20 percent. That kind of charge tacked on to your bills can quickly drain away any money you dreamed of investing. Think of a credit card balance as a guaranteed losing invest-ment.

It used to be that you needed a full-time job to qualify for a credit card, so most consumers didn't get cards until they were into their twenties. But these days teens are routinely offered cards. Mark Amantia, a New Jersey middle school social studies teacher, reports that a group of his seventh grade students who had participated in a stock market game all received credit card offers addressed to them at the school. While kids can't legally

better, a guaranteed minimum rate set by the government or the current market rate. Others earn the market rate without any guarantees. But the market rate also has been calculated differ-ently over the years. For Series EE bonds purchased from May 2000 to October 2000, the current interest rate is 5.73 percent. (Rates are adjusted every November and May.) To find out pre-cisely what interest rate a bond you own is now earning, I again refer you to the Treasury Web site for information.

Bonds grow in value continually until the day they "mature" and are worth face value. After that, they continue to earn interest, and their value continues to increase for years. But at some point they do max out. Series EE bonds earn interest for get cards until they're eighteen, some credit card issuers are now promoting credit cards in kids' names that parents sign for and are responsible for paying the bills on. It sounds like a great idea at first blush, but it's all too easy to indulge in impulse spending and get in way over your head.

Some 37 percent of eighteen- and nineteen-year-olds have credit cards in their own names, and as you go through college you'll probably find that you're bombarded with offers for cards. If you do choose to get a card, get in the habit of paying off each month's charges immediately, and use the card for convenience, not to buy everything you ever wanted. There's no doubt that credit cards are almost a necessity in adult American life. But if you get into financial trouble with credit cards when you're young, it will dog you for years. Use a card wisely, and you'll be rewarded with a good credit record (enabling you to get a mortgage or car loan someday) and with the 18 percent you didn't have to pay to credit card companies.

thirty years. After that, you're floating a free loan to Uncle Sam. Some of the old Series E bonds, no longer available, earn interest for forty years.

Another tricky thing about bonds is the science of when to cash them in. If your bond was bought after May 1997, it increases in value every month. If you're going to cash it in and invest that money elsewhere, you should cash it soon after the first of any month. (A warning, however: if you cash in bonds bought after May 1997 before they are five years old, you lose the last three months of interest.) If your bond was bought before May 1, 1997, it increases in value every six months. So if your bond was bought in January, it increases in value every

January 1 and July 1. If you cash a bond on June 30, you won't get any more than you would have back in January. (Another exception: bonds issued from March 1993 through April 1995 increase every month for the first five years only, then on a twice-a-year basis. See what I mean about the Treasury Department's fiddling?)

You don't owe any state or local taxes on the interest earned on savings bonds.

You do owe federal tax. You can choose one of two ways to report and pay the tax. (1) If you have some weird desire to torture yourself with increased paperwork, you can report the interest earned each year on your tax return, even though you haven't actually received any of that interest in the form of cash in your pocket. You have to consult government publications for more detailed instructions on how to do this. (2) Or you can wait to report the interest income when you cash out the bond, which is the method that most sane people use. The interest is then included with other interest income on your tax return for that year. (The bookkeeping is a nightmare the other way: for one thing, the Internal Revenue Service assumes you'll report it all when you cash in the bond, so you have to present your records to show that you've been paying all along.) If you want, you can roll over your bond—in other words, immediately buy another bond with the proceeds of the bond you're cashing in. This too is tricky. That's another job for that super Web site, **www.savingsbonds.gov**!

Something called the Education Savings Bond Program gives you or your parents a federal tax break on savings bonds used to pay for college or vocational school. There are several qualifications for the program, including two biggies: Series EE bonds must have been bought after January 1, 1990, and if your family earns too much income, you don't qualify for the tax break. The income limit is $78,350 for married couples and $52,250 for single filers.

Let's get to what I know you've been wanting to find out all along: how can you tell how much your savings bond is currently worth? You need to know three things: the series (such as EE); the issue date, which means when it was bought; and how much it is for—$50, $100, whatever. With this information, you can go to that same government Web site I've been referring you to (www.savingsbonds.gov). Once there, click on "online value calculator," which will ask you for the vital information and compute the value of your bond. This is a truly cool tool and just the kind of thing that the Internet does best: interactive information on demand. I used the calculator to value a couple of bonds I dug out of a file cabinet at my house and was fascinated to learn their worth. Here's what I found:

> STREET SLANG

THE TAPE

In your grandparents' day, ticker tape was **a thin strip of paper** that came out of a small printer and **listed the latest stock prices.** The old-style **"ticker tape parade"** was just that—a parade where the confetti was made up of ticker tape. Now the stock prices come from a computer, and there's precious little paper involved. But the name has endured. If you hear someone talking about "the tape," it means the latest listing of stock prices and trades.

•A $50 bond given to one of my kids in September 1997 is currently worth $27.92. It has a long way to go before even reaching maturity.

•A $50 bond given to another child in April 1987 is now worth $51.84. It has reached maturity—but only barely.

•A $50 bond given to my husband in May 1974 is now worth $217.08!

•The biggest surprise was unearthing another $50 bond given in October 1961, currently worth $384.68. It's almost time to cash that one in. Since bonds issued then continue to earn interest for forty years (starting in 1965, this type of bond earns interest for only thirty years), it will earn as much as it ever will by October 2001. I can't help but feel that the last two bonds would be better invested in the stock market.

It may be that savings bonds you've received as gifts could provide a source of some investment capital for you to try your hand in the stock market. Talk with your parents about this, and check out what your bonds are currently worth.

IF YOU'VE EVER STUDIED ANOTHER LANGUAGE, THE FIRST thing you may remember tackling is the alphabet. Before you can speak Spanish like a native, you need to know what the alphabet sounds like and what it looks like. Then you learn some basic words and phrases and go from there. It's the same with any new topic, even investing. In this chapter, we've discussed some of the basic principles of investing and learned what stocks and bonds are.

In the next chapter, you'll learn the "advanced basics"—how to make decisions about where to invest your money.

"The stock market
is a summary of
people's views
about the future."

|

GLENN HUBBARD
COLUMBIA GRADUATE SCHOOL
OF BUSINESS

Stock Picking 102

STILL PAYING ATTENTION? YOUTH BEING WHAT IT IS, I'm sure you're getting itchy to know when we move on to the action—actually putting money into investments. But hold on. Before we address how to do that, there are a few more basics you need to know. After all, plunking down your cash without learning something about choosing a stock would be a little like landing in a foreign country without a map or phrase book. You'd find yourself wandering around the city clueless—or in this case, wandering through the stock market clueless. In either place, you'd be vulnerable to getting ripped off.

HOW TO PICK A STOCK

THERE ARE MORE THAN 10,000 STOCKS OUT THERE IN THE universe of investable securities, and it can be plenty daunting to try to pick them. Where do you start?

Many people start by taking a look at the companies they encounter during their daily life. When you wake up in the morning, you may put on some clothing you bought at the Gap, eat a General Mills breakfast cereal, catch up with the news on *The Today Show* (part of General Electric), and get a ride to school in your dad's Ford. All of these are public companies in which you could become a part owner by buying stock.

Peter Lynch, the legendary author and former manager of Fidelity's Magellan mutual fund, has for years written about and championed the idea that ordinary investors can prosper in the market by taking note of which products and companies they are impressed by and using that as a starting point for investment ideas. As a teenager, you're uniquely situated to do that. Adults tend to get stuck in patterns, using the same products and being exposed to the same cultural influences year after year. Teens are famous for spotting trends and for being alert to what's new. In fact teens not only spot trends, they start them. One sixteen-year-old girl from Baraboo, Wisconsin, we spoke with thought of her best investing idea—which she used successfully in a stock market contest—by working in the toy department at Wal-Mart. She noticed some new toys were selling like crazy and figured out how to prosper from the Pokemon craze back when the fad was just heating up by investing in the company that had the licensing rights to the characters.

"My younger brother would trade stocks in video game companies when he was twelve or thirteen," says Jonathan Steinberg, chairman, chief executive officer, and founder of Individual Investor Group, which publishes *Individual Investor* magazine. "He went through different games, Atari and the rest, and when he felt the game was going stale and it was time to move on to the newer ones, he'd trade the stock, too. You have to play to your strengths and your interests. If you're interested in cars, read the annual reports of the automakers;

if you're a technology person, look at those companies."

Other investors get their ideas from the people around them. There's nothing wrong with listening to a friend's hot tip, as long as you check it out independently before buying. Reading the financial pages of your local newspaper, checking out financial Internet sites, and reading business magazines all will generate numerous stock ideas.

There are more methodical ways to get stock ideas. Many Internet sites have stock screening programs that allow you to set certain statistical parameters and check to see which companies conform to your specifications. For instance, you can ask a stock screening program to look for companies that have less than $200 million in revenues, annual sales growth of 15 percent or more, and stock prices less than $50 a share. The program will kick out a list of companies that you can then do a little more research on. (See "Teen Tool: Stock Sifting," on the following page.)

Before you buy a stock, you need to do some research and homework on it.

First, you need to become acquainted with the company and its business. What does the company produce? Is it in an industry that is thriving and that has the potential to do well in the coming years? Is the company's management respected? Is the company staying ahead of the competition?

Other information can be learned by looking at a company's financial reports:

>> **Is the company's business growing?** A steady growth in revenues and in profits over the past five years that is projected to continue is a positive sign. Remember, generally revenues or sales are how much money the company is taking into the corporate cash register, while profits or income is what is left after paying all the company's expenses.

>> **How does the company compare to others in its industry?** The best barometer of this is a statistic called **return on**

Teen Tool: Stock Sifting

WHERE DO I START? Many investors have a tough time figuring out where to begin looking for stocks. A stock screening program is one tool you can use to try to generate some ideas. In a stock screening program—made possible by the awesome brainpower of computers—you give guidelines for groups of stocks you're interested in, and it will search the stock market universe for stocks that fit your specifications. Stock screening programs are offered by Internet sites like AOL (**www.aol.com**), Motley Fool (**www.motleyfool.com**), Yahoo! Finance (**quote. yahoo.com**), and CBS Marketwatch (**www.marketwatch. com**).

To give you a better idea of what's involved, we've run a sample stock screen, using a Bloomberg stock screening program designed for professionals. We asked to see stocks that fit the following criteria: companies with (1) sales over $1 billion; (2) stock prices between $50 and $100 a share; (3) five-year average sales growth rates of at least 10 percent; and (4) five-year average profit growth rates of at least 10 percent. At right are the sixteen stocks that came up when the computer searched. A list like this can give you a jumping-off point for your stock picking.

equity (ROE). This will help tell you how good a job the corporate executives did in using the company's resources. Below are details on how to figure ROE. A good company will have a higher ROE than others in its industry; in any case, you want to see a return of 10 to 15 percent.

>> **Is the stock overpriced?** One measure of this is the price/earnings ratio. (See page 51 for an explanation of a price/earnings ratio.)

TICKER SYMBOL	COMPANY	BUSINESS
AA	Alcoa	Aluminum maker
BBY	Best Buy Co.	Consumer electronics retailing
CAH	Cardinal Health	Medical products wholesaler
CAT	Caterpillar Inc.	Farm and construction equipment
COST	Costco Wholesale	Discount retailer
FNM	Fannie Mae	Mortgage securities
FD	Federated Dept. Stores	Department stores
HD	Home Depot	Home improvement retailer
INTC	Intel	Computer chip maker
JCI	Johnson Controls	Automotive parts maker
JNJ	Johnson & Johnson	Pharmaceutical company
LOW	Lowe's Companies	Home improvement retailer
MRK	Merck & Co.	Pharmaceutical company
SUNW	Sun Microsystems	Computer network products and services
WMT	Wal-Mart	Discount retailer
WLA	Warner Lambert	Pharmaceutical company

>>**If the stock seems cheap, why?** Is it a company that has fallen out of favor with investors? Is it on the comeback trail, or is it just starting to decline?

>> **Is the company burdened by debt?** Just as high debt can hurt your personal finances, so it can hamper a company's. You'll want to look for the **book value** of a company, which tells you how much its assets minus its debt are worth; a low book value could mean it is carrying too much debt.

To get this kind of information, you can check out publications like *Value Line* or *Standard and Poor's* at your local library, or go online to various financial sites. (See Chapter 10 for the addresses of useful Web sites.) Most companies have investor relations departments that will also happily send you an annual report. If you or your parents have accounts at some of the big securities firms, like Merrill Lynch, Morgan Stanley Dean Witter, or Salomon Smith Barney, you have access to reports issued by securities analysts, whose job is to study and pick stocks. Ask your parents to call their broker and find out whether the firm has issued research reports on any of the companies you are interested in.

"I get my ideas about stocks from all sorts of places," says Matt Hooker, a twenty-year-old Notre Dame finance major who began getting interested in the stock market at age fifteen. "Sometimes my dad hears about a stock from a friend or from his broker. I also read *The Wall Street Journal* and magazines like *SmartMoney*. Sometimes I watch CNBC or MSNBC. After I have an idea I go online, to either Datek or CNNfn, and I look at how analysts rate the stock. I'm also looking at estimates of future growth. I'm not interested in dividend yield." Hooker's successful stock picks have included Pfizer and America Online.

Once in a while in your stock-picking career, you may pick a grand-slam stock—one that shows up on lists of biggest gainers. Congratulations. It's a terrific achievement. You've earned some bragging rights (limited bragging rights, please) and had the excitement of watching your stock take a nice run. But it's easy to be blinded by the stock market supernovas and forget that it is possible to be an extremely successful investor without picking the next Amazon.com or CMGI. Remember, the tortoise won the race.

THE TWO MAJOR KINDS OF STOCK ANALYSIS

IN WRITING HOW TO PICK STOCKS ABOVE, I HAVE DESCRIBED what's known as **fundamental analysis.** It involves evaluating companies, then trying to figure out whether a stock is cheap or expensive when you look at the underlying worth of the company and its expected future earnings. Fundamental research is the traditional method of security analysis. The most famous fundamentalist was probably Benjamin Graham, a Columbia University business school professor who wrote a basic textbook on security analysis back in 1934 and a best-selling investing book, *The Intelligent Investor,* in 1949 that remains one of the most respected financial guidebooks ever. Graham's best known pupil is legendary investor Warren Buffett.

The other main variety of stock analysis is **technical analysis.** Technical analysis looks only at stock price movements in trying to predict which shares might see a rise, reasoning that any useful information about the company has already been incorporated into the stock price. Technical analysts look at historical price trends in any given stock, trading volume (how many shares are bought and sold in any given day), the ratio of how many stocks went up that day to how many went down, and other factors. Because they plot data using charts to decipher the market, technical analysts are often called **technicians** or **chartists**. The analysts may look at a company's trading pattern to try to discern the support level of a stock or the resistance level—the price at which the stock doesn't usually trade below

> ## >STREET SMARTS
>
> The company listed longest on the New York Stock Exchange is **Consolidated Edison Co. of New York.** It was first listed as **New York Gas Light Company** in 1824.
>
> SOURCE: NEW YORK STOCK EXCHANGE

49 < <

or above. Some technical analysts like to brag that they don't even need to know what business a company is in or who runs it in order to read its future from its historical price movements.

Many people use a combination of fundamental and technical analysis in investing, saying that fundamental analysis can help you decide *what* to buy and technical analysis can tell you *when* to buy.

WHAT'S A STOCK SPLIT?

THE SHORT ANSWER IS, IT'S A GOOD THING. LET'S GO BACK and take a quick look at Sole Survivor, your booming athletic shoe company. Remember, you've gone public, and your stock is climbing nicely on the New York Stock Exchange. The price has hit $100 a share. But you think that perhaps the stock price is getting beyond the reach of ordinary individual investors. When that happens, you declare a stock split. If it's a two-for-one split, for instance, each investor will get two shares for every one they own. These shares will now be worth $50 each. While investors haven't immediately made any money, stock splits are usually indicative of a thriving company, and the stock price will tend to creep back up to higher levels.

A FEW IMPORTANT FINANCIAL CALCULATIONS

NO GROANS, PLEASE. THESE ARE SHORT, EASY, AND ESSENtial. Although you won't have to do the actual calculations often—these statistics are easily available from *Value Line*, Standard and Poor's, and other basic investment resources—it's a good idea to know what goes into these numbers.

>>**Earnings Per Share (EPS).** Just as it sounds. The company's net earnings are divided by the number of shares of stock

outstanding to get EPS. You're looking for a number that keeps going up each year.

>>**Price/Earnings Ratio.** The price/earnings (P/E) ratio is one of the more popular measurements of a stock price. It is calculated by dividing the stock price by the company's earnings per share over the past year. In recent years, it has become more common for analysts to look at a company's expected earnings per share over the coming year also. The P/E is easy to calculate, although the newspaper stock pages usually list it, and it's certainly available on any Internet site worth a click. You can use the P/E ratio to compare companies within industries to try to figure out whether the stock is overpriced. (It doesn't do much good to compare steel companies with Internet companies.) Some-

> **>STREET SMARTS**
> •Average P/E ratio of S&P 500 stocks in 1989: **16**
> •Average P/E ratio of S&P 500 stocks in 1999: **31**

times you hear this expressed as "times earnings," as in "Warner Lambert is selling at thirty times earnings." The average P/E ratio for stocks on the Standard and Poor's 500 is currently about thirty-one; that's up markedly from more historical averages of about fifteen.

A big debate is going on in financial circles about whether the high P/E ratios—especially in Internet stocks—mean that the whole stock market is overheated or whether there has been some kind of fundamental shift in what acceptable P/E ratios should be. Time will tell, to paraphrase half the financial forecasting community!

>>**Return on Equity (ROE).** This number is like a corporate management final grade: it tells how well management invests its own resources. For the most part, you're looking for companies with an ROE of at least 10 to 15 percent.

Buy, Sell, or Hold: Amazon Dilemma

HOW LONG TO HOLD AMAZON (AMZN) is the question that twenty-two-year-old investor Gregg Fidan found himself asking not long ago. The Internet book retailer has been a darling of day traders and online investors because of its prominence and dominance in its industry. In 1997 it was selling for less than $5 a share. Fidan bought Amazon at 95 in the spring of 1999 and watched it quickly shoot up to 110. He thought about selling, didn't, and watched it drop back quickly to 90.

In the summer of 1999, again he wondered: should he sell and cut his losses in this company that has yet to make a profit, or should he hold on?

What he did: Fidan decided to hold. "When it went back down to 90, I had a pretty bad feeling in my stomach, but I still think if you buy and hold good quality Internet companies, you'll see the stocks go up. My target is five or even ten years out. I don't think there will be as many Internet companies as there are today, and I think Amazon will be a force in the Internet," says Fidan, who created an Internet site while a student at North Carolina State and sold it to the company he now works for, Cosmoz.com.

What has happened: So far, Fidan made the right call. Since he decided to hold, Amazon has rewarded stockholders with a two-for-one stock split and is currently trading at about 62, a nice profit from his original position. Not that he's thinking of cashing in—Fidan says he'll stick with his five-to-ten-year timetable for this stock.

KINDS OF STOCKS

DIFFERENT TERMS ARE USED TO DESCRIBE STOCKS, AS YOU'LL see by some of the labels listed below. These are unofficial terms—no regulatory agency designates that certain stocks are "growth" stocks or "income" stocks. Nevertheless, these terms are used to explain characteristics of stocks. You will see them used when you read about companies, and it's useful to know what they mean.

Growth stocks are bought because the investor thinks the company will grow rapidly, leading to a rise in the stock price.

Income stocks are ones that are bought—at least in part—for their dividends.

Over-the-counter (OTC) stocks refers to where the stocks are traded. OTC means they are traded on Nasdaq, the computerized network that matches sellers and buyers (unlike the New York Stock Exchange, which is a real bricks-and-mortar building and trading floor). OTC stocks tend to be smaller companies, and many high-technology companies are listed on Nasdaq, including Microsoft.

>STREET SLANG

DEAD-CAT BOUNCE
Bear with me, animal lovers. Even a dead cat, if it falls from high enough, will bounce upon hitting the ground. Likewise with a dead stock: **the price may rebound after hitting a low, but,** as with our deceased feline, **it's not going to stay up.**

Penny stocks are ones that sell for less than $1 or $5 a share (investors draw the line at different places). But everyone agrees that penny stocks are small businesses, and they are often high-risk investments. Penny stocks also have been notorious for being easily and illegally manipulated.

In the terms **large-cap stocks** and **small-cap stocks,** cap refers to the company's market capitalization. (There are also **mid-cap** stocks, to round out the field.) To calculate market capitalization, multiply the number of outstanding shares by the share price. Although how much it takes to be considered large cap varies depending on who you talk to, generally large caps are companies that have a market capitalization over $3.5 billion; small caps have somewhere between $250 million and $1 billion. Below $250 million is considered **microcap**. Investors have different reasons for liking companies with different size capitalizations. Many people feel large-cap companies are more stable and their stock price is less likely to fluctuate greatly. Smaller-cap companies are more likely to see higher rates of growth, since they are still in the early years of their life cycle. Smaller companies also are preferred by some bargain hunters who think that small companies may be relatively undiscovered because they may not have been the focus of so much attention on Wall Street.

INVESTING STYLES

FEW INDIVIDUAL INVESTORS ARE STRICT PUREBREDS IN investing styles; most tend to be stock market mutts, combining a couple of strategies. A couple of the most common investment philosophies are outlined below.

>>**Growth investor.** A growth investor is someone who looks for companies that expect their sales and profits to grow faster than the economy, and faster than most other companies. The growth investor reasons that the earnings growth will fuel a stock price rise. The danger: what goes up can come down.

>>**Value investor.** This can be a bit of a misleading term. Who isn't looking for value in everything, including stocks? (Can't you just hear a professional money manager telling a client, "No, I don't believe in looking for value"?)
But in stock market and investing terms, being a value

investor means looking for and investing in companies that, for whatever reason, have cheap stock prices, below their intrinsic value. These stocks usually have low P/E ratios and higher dividend yields than growth stocks. The idea is that you're getting a bargain. The danger, of course, is that the stock may stay a bargain indefinitely.

>>**Momentum investor.** This is someone who looks for stocks that are on the move up and tries to jump on for the ride. This is, almost by definition, a strategy for short-term trading rather than for buy-and-hold investors. Some momentum investors look for stock prices that are rising; others look for companies that are on a roll from repeated earnings increases. The danger: despite science's best efforts, there is no such thing as a perpetual motion machine, and that goes for the market as well. Even fast-moving stocks can run out of steam.

HIGH-OCTANE INVESTING

YOU KNOW THE WARNINGS THAT ADVERTISERS PUT ON THOSE car commercials? The ones that warn you not to try the stunt-driving techniques at home? Similar warnings should be posted for the novice considering some of the stock-trading strategies below. These trading techniques are risky and not for beginners, but once you feel comfortable with the basics of investing, you may want to learn more.

>>**Margin.** Buying on margin involves buying stock with borrowed money. You're allowed to borrow up to 50 percent of the stock price of your holdings to buy more stock. (Some brokerage firms may enforce more stringent margin rules.) If your portfolio is worth $10,000, you can borrow up to $5,000 to buy more stock. You're leveraging your assets, and the strategy can pay off.

But if the value of your holdings ever drops, you will receive a **margin call** from your broker. The margin call is rightly dreaded by both brokers and customers. It means that the value of your portfolio has dropped and therefore can't serve as collateral for as large a loan. If your $10,000 worth of stocks dropped in value to $8,000, you could borrow a maximum of $4,000 against that. If you had an outstanding margin position of $5,000, you would have to come up with another $1,000 in cash or assets to continue to support your $5,000 loan. If you couldn't, the broker would simply sell part of your portfolio. These are not fun phone calls for either brokers or their investor customers. ("Hi, remember that stock I recommended you borrow to buy? It's dropped so far that you have to send us more money" is roughly the message the broker has to give the customer.)

As with any loan, the brokerage firm will charge you interest for borrowing on margin to buy more stock. Currently the going rate on margin loans is about 8 percent.

SELLING SHORT

SHORT SELLING IS A WAY TO MAKE MONEY WHEN THE MARKET is going down—or at least when some of the stocks are. It involves selling stocks you don't yet own, in an attempt to profit from that stock's expected drop in price. Technically you are borrowing the stocks when you sell short and have to buy them later.

When would you use short selling? Let's say you're convinced that your favorite fast-food company's stock is going to drop. (You've just come back from a food run and have serious doubts about that creamed spinach sandwich they're introducing.) You might short their shares at $30 a share, convinced they're going lower. If you're right and the stock drops to $20, you've made $10 per share, a nice little profit. What happens then is you buy the stock at $20 to cover your short position—in effect, you buy at $20 what you've already sold at $30.

There are a couple of things to remember about selling short. If you're wrong in your guess and the stock price starts to climb, it can really cost you to cover your position. If you buy a stock in the usual way, the most money you can lose is the total of what you paid for it. If you sell short, the price can keep climbing and climbing endlessly—in which case your losses also climb and climb, until you cover your position. Short selling is not for weak stomachs and is not recommended for beginning—or even very experienced—investors.

READING THE STOCK TABLES IN THE NEWSPAPER

YOU CAN FIND STOCK PRICES STREAMING ACROSS THE BOTtom of your television screen and the Web sites you visit, but for portability and convenience, nothing beats the stock pages of *The Wall Street Journal* or your local newspaper. Stock tables give the previous business day's stock prices at the close of the day, so in the *Journal,* for example, Friday's closing prices will appear in Monday's paper. You need to look at the correct stock table to find your stock: a Nasdaq stock is listed under the Nasdaq pages and a New York Stock Exchange stock is listed with the results of all of the other NYSE stocks. How can you decode all those columns of data? Below is a listing from a day's trading of Walt Disney Co., the theme park and entertainment company.

52 Week High	Low	Stock	Div.	Yld %	P/E	Sales 100s	High	Low	Last	Chg
$41^{15}/_{16}$	$23^{3}/_{8}$	DIS	.21	.5	83	65398	$41^{3}/_{4}$	$41^{1}/_{16}$	$41^{3}/_{8}$	$-^{3}/_{16}$

>>**52 Week High/Low.** The highest and lowest prices paid for that stock during the past year. $41^{15}/_{16}$ equals 41.9375 and $23^{3}/_{8}$ equals 23.375. There is a plan to replace the fractions with

The Dow Closed Up Today

IF YOU TURN ON THE NIGHTLY NEWS, YOU CAN'T ESCAPE mention of the Dow, short for the Dow Jones Industrial Average (DJIA). Network anchors solemnly recite the closing Dow every weeknight, and when the Dow hit 10,000 a while back, it was big news.

What is the Dow, anyway? It's the short answer to the question "What happened in the stock market today?" The DJIA is an index that tracks the stock performance of thirty leading companies, including such firms as Coca-Cola, Exxon, American Express, and General Electric. It takes the closing stock prices of those companies, adds them, and then divides the sum by a number that is statistically computed to avoid the distorting effect of stock splits. If you're curious about what other companies are in the DJIA, take a look at Chapter 7, pages 142–143.

But the Dow isn't the only useful index to know—in fact,

decimals, so you'd pay 41.93 or 41.94 for a stock, although at this writing, that change has been postponed.

>>**Stock.** The name of the company. Companies are listed alphabetically. Depending on how much room the paper has, it may use a ticker symbol or it may spell out or abbreviate the name in another way.

>>**Div.** Dividend. For each share of stock owned, a shareholder received 21 cents from Disney's profit last year. Dividends are often paid quarterly, although the figure given is an annual figure. If this space is blank, there is no dividend. Newer companies often don't pay dividends.

many observers think that other indices are actually more descriptive of what the market did. Dow Jones itself does have other indices, but after the DJIA, the best known is the Standard and Poor's 500 index, or the S&P 500.

Obviously the S&P 500 tracks a much larger group of companies than does the DJIA and has tremendous influence, but the Wilshire 5000 Equity Index (Wilshire 5000) tracks an even larger group, including NYSE and American Stock Exchange stocks as well as most of the more active Nasdaq stocks. The Russell 2000 tracks small-company stocks, and the Nasdaq composite index measures that exchange's 4,825 stocks (see **www.nasdaq.com** for a complete listing).

You'll also hear foreign indices discussed, like the Tokyo stock market's Nikkei average, London's Financial Times Stock Exchange average (the FTSE 100, pronounced "footsie"), and Hong Kong's Hang Seng index.

>>Yld %. Percent yield. The percent yield shows the rate of return that the 21 cents per share dividend represents on the current price of the stock. Disney's yield here is 0.5 percent, a lower rate than you could find even on a savings account. (Although remember, dividends are only part of how investors earn money on stocks; an escalating stock price usually produces a higher return on stocks than the dividend.)

>>P/E. Price/Earnings Ratio. The price/earnings ratio shows the price of a single share of stock divided by the company's earnings per share for the last year. The higher the P/E, the more stockholders are paying for each dollar of company earnings.

The Major Indices

HERE IS HOW the world's major stock market indices closed out the last century. Below are their closing prices for 1999.

INDEX	YEAR-END LEVEL
Dow Jones Industrial Average	11,497.12
S&P 500	1,469.25
Wilshire 5000	13,812.7
Russell 2000	504.75
Nasdaq Composite	4,069.31
Nikkei	18,934.34
FTSE 100	6,930.2
Hang Seng	16,962.1

>>**Sales 100s.** The sales 100s figure shows you how much of this stock traded yesterday. On this day, 6,539,800 shares traded. Heavy trading can be triggered by good or bad news announced by the company. In some newspapers, if there is the letter "f" next to the volume figure, it means that four zeros have been omitted, not two. If there is a "z" next to the figure, it means that the actual number shown been traded with no zeros omitted.

>>**High.** This shows the highest price paid for the stock the previous day, in this case, 41.75 per share.

>>**Low.** This shows the lowest price paid during the previous day, in this case, 41.0625.

>>**Last.** This shows the last price paid at the close of the trading day. In this case, Disney closed at 41.375.

>>**Chg.** This shows how much the closing price was above or below the previous day's price. In this case, it was down -³⁄₁₆, or .1875 cents per share. In some newspapers, if the price changes by more than 5 percent in either direction, the quote is printed in boldface to highlight it.

OPTIONS: PUTS AND CALLS

OPTIONS ARE CLEARLY FOR THE SOPHISTICATED INVESTOR. Many successful and respected investors never deal in options, and you, too, can feel free to skip over this section. But I have noticed that there is an interest in options on the part of some teens—particularly those who participate in some of the stock market investing contests (more on this in Chapter 9). Below is a quick primer on options.

The appeal to options is their leverage. If all goes well (and, of course, that's a big if), you can make a much higher return on your cash by trading options on a stock than by buying and selling the stock itself.

Here are the formal definitions of call options and put options: A **call option** gives the buyer the right—but not the obligation—to buy an asset at a fixed price during a specific period of time. A **put option** is the flip side. It gives the buyer the right (but again, not the obligation) to sell an asset at a fixed price during a specific period of time.

In plain language, here's how an **equity option** would work. (There are also index options, but we're going to ignore them for now.) Let's say you think a stock is headed up. Pretend Exxon is now trading for $50 (as this is being written, it's trading for a good bit more than that). You could, of course, buy Exxon stock. But another angle, which allows you to leverage your available cash a little more, would involve call options. You might buy a call option for $5 that gives you the right to buy the stock at $70 a share. (That's called the **strike price.)** Let's say you buy the Exxon option, and you are correct about the stock going up: It soars to $85 a share. You exercise your option, buy the stock at $70 a share, then immediately sell it at the going price of $85. Your profit (before taxes, of course): $15 per share. Your out-of-pocket cash investment: $5. If you had bought the stock outright, your profit would have been $35 on a cash investment of $50. Not bad, certainly, but not the profit multiple of the option. That's called **leverage.**

Put options work in reverse. Let's say you've lost faith in Exxon. You buy a put option, believing that Exxon, at $50, is going down. If you're right, and the stock drops to $30, you exercise your option of selling it at $40, which you can do profitably because you can now buy it for $30. Again, a nice little profit.

With both puts and calls, you don't have to actually exercise the option by buying and selling stock: the option itself can be—and usually is—bought and sold. Each option contract represents 100 shares of stock, so twenty Exxon contracts would represent 2,000 shares.

Your option comes with an expiration date; the longer the time period before it expires, the more the put or call option costs. Typical option periods are three months, although there are longer periods. The prices of options vary through the life of the option; if things are looking good for the stock, call options may become more expensive. After its expiration date, an option is worth nothing. (Unlike a bond, for instance, which matures on a certain date.) If you're lucky enough to have an unexpired option that already could be exercised for a profit (say your Exxon call option is trading at $75 a share with a couple of weeks to go before expiration), you have an "in-the-money" option.

In addition to being a pure speculator's game, options can be used as a sort of insurance against losses. Let's say you own Exxon stock, and you don't think the stock price is going to rise dramatically. You could "write" a "covered call" on your stock and make some extra money by being paid the **premium** (another name for the price of the option). "Covered" refers to the fact that you already own the stock. Writing calls on stock you don't own is dubbed a "naked call" and is extremely risky, since the potential losses can be very high. If the stock does rise, you won't reap the full appreciation on it; you'll earn only the strike price in the call option. The rest of the profit goes to the buyer of the call.

So options can provide both a speculative kick to your investments (to the buyer of puts and calls) and a bit of insurance (to the writer, or stock-owning seller, of a call). But options should be considered a sophisticated strategy to be used only when you feel comfortable with regular stock buying and selling, have mastered the methods of doing research on stocks, and really have extra money to play with. To make money in options you have to be right not only about which stocks are going to move and what direction they will move in but also about *when* they are going to move. If your timing is slightly off, your options can expire worthless.

> **>STREET SLANG**
> **SUCKERS' RALLY**
> After a drop in stock prices, the market turns up again. But those in the know realize that **prices are headed back down, so they sell into a suckers' rally.**

And don't forget, as with stock trading, there are commissions to be paid every time you buy or write options. Any profit calculations must take that into account. Options are traded on many but not all stocks. Option prices are listed in the financial pages of newspapers, just as stock prices are.

Determining whether option prices are over- or undervalued is such a complicated task that the mathematical brains who devised a formula to do so won a Nobel Prize in economics for their achievement. The Black-Scholes model for pricing options takes into account such variables as the price of the underlying

Ticker Talk

IT SEEMS LIKE EVERYWHERE YOU LOOK YOU SEE STOCK tickers. They run across the bottom of the TV screen if you watch financial news shows, such as those on CNBC. They run across the front of buildings in the downtown districts of large cities. To the uninformed, the ticker makes no more sense than Egyptian hieroglyphics. But to the Street wise, it tells you how your stock portfolio is doing.

Each company has a ticker symbol, of anywhere from one to four letters. It's clear what companies some of these represent (IBM's ticker symbol is . . . IBM!) while others are either obscure or funny. More later on the funny ones. But for now let's look at, say, GM, the ticker symbol for General Motors.

Ticker symbols with three or fewer letters are listed on the New York Stock Exchange (NYSE) or the American Stock Exchange. Think GM, IBM, or XOM, the new symbol for the merged Exxon-Mobil. Ticker symbols with four letters are companies that are listed on Nasdaq. Think INTC (Intel) or MSFT (Microsoft). If a company has different classes of stocks, you may see an A or B after the stock symbol.

A company's ticker symbol is followed by a recent stock price. That price is a whole number, followed, if necessary, by a fraction. At this writing stocks are priced in increments of 1/16 of a dollar. One-sixteenth is worth $.0625, two-sixteenths is worth $.125, and so on. The stock market is scheduled to try "decimalization" later in the year 2000. At first stock prices will trade in increments of $.05, and then eventually, it is hoped, in increments of $.01. What a welcome simplification that will be for investors!

So you might see GM scroll across the ticker with the numbers 72 15/16, which tells you General Motors is trading at $72.94 for a share of stock. This may also be shown as 72 ' 15.

In this case, the sixteenths is assumed. If you see a 72 3 without an apostrophe, it means that the stock price is calibrated in eighths. (That decimalization can't get here fast enough for me.)

Often after the number you'll see an up or down arrow, telling you whether the most recent price has risen or fallen, or sometimes a plus or minus sign with a number, to tell you how much the price has risen or fallen. Some tickers even show rising stocks in a reassuring, money-green color and falling stocks in an alarming red so you can quickly tell how the tape is running.

Companies choose their ticker symbol. There are some guidelines; two companies can't have the same symbol, obviously. A few stocks on the NYSE are represented by single letters: Ford Motor Company is simply F, while AT&T is just A. But company ticker symbols can also tell you what sort of business the company is in. Cannondale Bicycle Company's symbol is BIKE, and brewer Anheuser Busch is BUD. Other symbols are misleading. The hip retailer the Gap isn't GAP but GPS. That's because GAP belongs to Great Atlantic and Pacific, better known as A&P supermarkets.

And still other ticker symbols convey another message: that their executives have a sense of humor. Sunglasses maker Oakley has the ticker symbol OO, which is supposed to resemble a pair of eyes. Internet America's execs are proud to call themselves GEEK on the ticker, while Southwest Airlines has the symbol LUV, because the Dallas airport, Love Field, is where many of its flights begin. Vermont Teddy Bear's BEAR symbol and California Culinary Academy's COOK are tip-offs as to what the companies do and easy for an investor to remember.

But as clever as these symbols are, don't choose investments solely by the ticker symbol. After all, the dismal results might well drive you BATS (Batteries Batteries, battery distributors).

stock, the strike price of the option, when the option expires, how much you could earn in risk-free investments, and how much the stock has tended to fluctuate in the past. Even with this model there are still uncertainties—no one can know how a stock will fluctuate in the future. As you might guess, there are computer software programs that use the Black-Scholes formulas. But the intricacies of pricing and trading options are a bit more complicated than we're going to get into in this book.

OTHER PLACES WE'RE NOT TRAVELING TO TODAY

OPTIONS ARE EXAMPLES OF **DERIVATIVES**—SECURITIES THAT get their value from that of an underlying asset or an underlying benchmark. Other types of derivatives you may hear about include index futures and Standard and Poor's 500 Depository Receipts (SPDRs). More are being invented by Wall Street firms every day.

My position on derivatives is that they are for sophisticated traders who can afford to lose some money. So are futures—like the pork-belly futures you hear about Chicago traders buying and selling or financial futures, such as Standard and Poor's 500 futures—and investment avenues like foreign currency trading.

Isn't it nice to know you have somewhere to graduate to after you've mastered the stock market?

"It is not the return *on* my investment I am worried about . . . it is the return *of* my investment."

WILL ROGERS

The Nuts and Bolts of Buying Stocks

YOU CAN STUDY THE STOCK MARKET ALL YOU WANT.
You can even draw up a "paper portfolio," keeping track of the performance of a group of stocks you're interested in. But there's nothing like having real money—your hard-earned money—invested in stocks to get your attention.

No doubt you're eager to get on with investing and to try what you've read about. This chapter will take you through the process step-by-step as well as give you some ideas on how your parents and grandparents might be able to assist you.

CUSTODIAL ACCOUNTS

UNFORTUNATELY, YOU CAN'T WALK INTO YOUR LOCAL MERRILL Lynch office or call up Charles Schwab and open an account. You're too young. An adult—most likely a parent—must open a

A Tip for Teens: You'll Be Sorry. . .

A COMMON NIGHTMARE parents have concerning custodial accounts is that they'll put money in an account for you, intending it to be used for college, graduate school, or some other worthy purpose, and you'll hit legal age, take the money, and buy a sports car, which you will, in short order, proceed to crash into a telephone pole. A variation on this nightmare has you donating the entire stash to some faddish cult you've fallen under the sway of.

I would say this: you have every legal right to do that. But don't. By the time you hit legal age, you should have figured out that money is easier spent than made, and if you blow this money, you will regret it for the rest of your life.

custodial account for you. Although you own the assets, your parent has control of the account. That's because a minor can't legally enter into a contract.

The formal names for custodial accounts—the acronyms you and your parents will see on the forms they fill out and sign—are UGMA and UTMA accounts. That stands for Uniform Gifts to Minors Act (UGMA) and Uniform Transfers to Minors Act (UTMA), after the laws that enabled these accounts to be set up.

An aside: I keep saying "your parents" here. For most kids, a parent or stepparent will be the person setting up such an account, but there's nothing in the law that says someone else can't. A grandparent, cousin, family friend, or some other adult can be the custodian. The person who has control over the account is the **custodian**, and you are the **beneficiary.**

The custodian sets up the account for you and has the authority to make all decisions concerning the account. But the money in it belongs to you and must be spent for your

A Tip for the Parents of a Teen: Breathe Easy

TO ADULTS, I HAVE A FEW POINTS to make. First of all, if the money in the custodial account is coming from you, there's no reason to transfer a lot of money into it. The tax benefits diminish (see "Taxes and More Taxes" on page 80), there can be college financial aid considerations (see "Custodial Accounts and College Financial Aid" on page 73), and there is the unchangeable fact that you will lose control over the money in a few years.

Having said that, I advise you to relax. Every financial planner I've ever asked about this over the course of several years tells me it's exceedingly rare for kids to squander the proceeds of a custodial account once they get their hands on it. Most kids do have some common sense by the time they're legal adults. If it really looks as if your kid might do something stupid, one strategy might be for you to spend the money—for his or her benefit, of course—before the kid is old enough to get at it. Pay for private school, summer school, tutoring, travel and study programs, or college costs directly out of the custodial account. You can't take the money back, nor can you use it to pay for normal support of a child (which is an ambiguous area), but you can spend it for the child's benefit.

As I mentioned before, laws vary from state to state. For more information on custodial accounts, a great source is the Web site of Kaye Thomas, a tax attorney and expert on custodial accounts: **www.fairmark.com.**

benefit, and at some point the account is turned over to you.

How old do you have to be before you can get control of the account? It varies from state to state. Some states specify that the beneficiary be eighteen; in others the custodian can choose another age—twenty-one is a common age specified. States will always have an upper limit on how old you can be.

One thing some parents misunderstand about a custodial account is this: once the money is in there, it belongs to the child. The custodian can't change his or her mind and take the money back. The income on the money also belongs to the beneficiary. (See "A Tip for Teens: You'll Be Sorry..." and "A Tip for the Parents of a Teen: Breathe Easy" on pages 70 and 71.)

CONTROL OF THE CUSTODIAL ACCOUNT

SO A CUSTODIAL ACCOUNT HAS BEEN SET UP IN YOUR BENEFIT, you have a few thousand dollars in it, and you're ready to trade.

There's one little hitch. You're not supposed to be the one giving a broker the buy and sell decisions on the account. The law is very clear on this. "A broker should not accept any direction from someone other than the custodian," says Kaye Thomas, a tax attorney and expert on custodial accounts. "The custodian is the one who makes the investment decisions and withdrawals and decides how the account is spent."

Brokerage firms are very clear about this, too, saying for the record that they don't accept orders from minors.

But who is kidding whom? How much latitude you have to buy and sell without your parents looking over your shoulder is between you and your parents, particularly with brokerage accounts that have online trading capabilities. "For our online accounts, we can't monitor who is placing the order," says Greg Gable, a spokesperson for Charles Schwab & Co. "If a teenager has the password, they have access to the account. In any case, with all trades in custodial accounts, confirmation slips go out by mail to the custodian, so parents will be notified about any trading."

And young traders tell of brokers accepting telephone orders from them, even though they're officially not supposed to. "I invested through a family broker; the broker knew it was OK with my dad if I did this," says Individual Investor Group's Jonathan Steinberg.

CUSTODIAL ACCOUNTS AND COLLEGE FINANCIAL AID

CUSTODIAL ACCOUNTS HAVE A DRAWBACK IF YOU ARE THINK-ing about applying for college financial aid. Under the current system, having a lot of money or stocks and mutual funds in a custodial account can reduce the amount of financial aid you qualify for.

That's because when assets are in a student's name, more of that money (under current formulas, about 35 percent) is assumed to be available to pay college expenses each year. Assets in a parent's name are tapped at only about 6 percent a year. You and your parents have to decide whether your family is likely to be eligible for need-based financial aid and then whether your stock account is going to be large enough to have an impact on your college aid. College financial aid is figured

> STREET SLANG

PAPER PROFIT (OR LOSS) Refers to the time **when a stock you own has made money (or lost it), but you haven't yet sold it,** so your gain or loss is still "on paper," only. Once you sell you're said to have "realized" a gain or loss. Ironically investors tend to think of paper profits as real but of paper losses as only on paper.

mostly on your parents' income (not assets), so you may not qualify for much student aid based on that alone.

It's also important to note that from time to time, bills have been introduced in Congress to change how financial aid is figured so that a parent's and a child's assets are combined when figuring family assets. Although the formulas remain the same at this writing, if such a change were made, it wouldn't much matter whose name the assets were in.

TRUSTS

IF YOUR FAMILY HAS BIG BUCKS AND WANTS TO TRANSFER tens of thousands of dollars to you, a custodial account probably isn't the best way to do it. A regular old trust is the way for your parents to go when big money—say, $50,000 or more—is being transferred. A trust allows parents to be more restrictive about when and how the money can be used by the kids. Ask your folks to consult your family attorney and accountants for details.

HOW TO BUY A STOCK

YOU CAN'T STOP BY THE FLOOR OF THE NEW YORK STOCK Exchange and order ten shares of GE; you have to go through a stockbroker, who transmits your order to the floor, where the stock is bought and sold. And so before you put any money on the line, you need to choose a stockbroker.

Full-Service Brokers

THINK OF STOCK BROKERAGE FIRMS (OR, AS THEY LIKE TO call themselves, financial services firms, since they do sell more than stock) as large stores. One luxurious store may have a large staff on hand to help recommend certain products, while another is a more bare-bones operation that requires customers to know what they want. And guess what? Just as it costs more to buy things at a fancy store than it does at a Sam's Club or other warehouse store, it costs more to buy and sell stock at a full-service firm. The price of the stock doesn't vary, but the per-share commission cost is higher at the full-service broker.

(**Commissions** are the fees charged for buying or selling a stock.)

Full-service brokers include such companies as Merrill Lynch, PaineWebber, and Salomon Smith Barney. Several well-known regional full-service firms do business in particular areas of the country, such as Edward Jones and Alex. Brown & Sons. (These firms are also called "wire houses.") Full-service brokers are more expensive because along with the stockbroker who deals directly with you (the customer), the firm has investment analysts who study and follow different industries and stocks.

Analysts issue research reports on the prospects of different companies. If a brokerage's analysts were to decide that, for instance, the business outlook for Intel or McDonald's was especially good or bad, they'd issue a buy or hold recommendation. Those investment analysts are supposed to provide the brainpower for the stockbroker recommending stocks. So when you pay higher commissions at the full-service brokers, what you're paying for is the research you have access to. You should consider using a full-service broker if you're the type of investor who needs to have someone tell you which stocks or mutual funds you should buy.

Your main contact at a full-service brokerage house is a **registered rep** (called that because the reps have to register with securities regulatory agencies) or financial adviser. That's the broker who calls you and recommends that you buy or sell certain stocks. Remember that a broker gets paid when you buy or sell stocks (and pay the commission). The best brokers get to know you and what kind of investing is good for you and make only smart, reasonable suggestions. The worst brokers push the "stock of the day" on customers to boost their commissions.

There are many good brokers out there, but it's important to always remember that a broker is primarily a stock salesperson. The typical line that brokers deliver to hesitant new customers is this: "I have an interest in seeing you do well. If you don't make money, I don't make money." Well, the truth is a little more complicated than that. Since brokers get paid on commission when you buy and sell, if you buy and hold and hold and hold—which is what many of the most successful investors do—the broker won't make money no matter how high your returns are. So while brokers like to have successful customers, what they need are customers who trade. Always keep this in the back of your mind when you're talking to a broker.

Discount Brokers

YEARS AGO I WANTED TO BUY AN EXPENSIVE CAMERA AS cheaply as possible. I went to a store in New York City—now out of business—that had a reputation for having the cheapest prices around. You stood in line in front of a counter, and when it was your turn you told the clerk exactly what make and model you wanted. They fetched it for you, and you paid up and went on your way. The man in front of me clearly didn't understand this operating system. When it was his turn, he told the clerk he was interested in a tripod. "What make? What model?" barked the clerk, a little more rudely than necessary. (Maybe the clerk's attitude had something to do with why they're now out of business.) At any rate, the rules were pretty clear: come back when you know exactly what you want.

Discount brokers operate this way—although with a lot more courtesy. These are the Charles Schwabs, the Fidelity Investments, and the Quick & Reillys of the world. They're for investors who know what they want. You don't call and ask whether they think Intel would be a good investment. You call, give them an order, and they execute it. In exchange, you get discount commission rates—as much as 45 percent cheaper than at full-service firms. Many discount firms offer such services as trading online and a variety of other investment products, such as mutual funds. If you feel you don't need the advice or hand-holding of a broker, and you do your own research (we'll tell you about resources for doing your own research in Chapter 10), a discount broker may be right for you.

And Then There Are the Deep Discounters

THESE GUYS OFFER EVEN FEWER SERVICES THAN DISCOUNT brokers like Fidelity or Charles Schwab, but they're also even cheaper—perhaps 65 percent cheaper than full-service firms. Deep discounters like Ceres Securities or National Discount Brokers appeal to very active, very independent investors.

When you're choosing a broker, compare the commission rates—they can vary depending on how much you buy and sell. Ask, too, what the minimum balance is for an account, and whether there are other fees involved, such as a maintenance fee if you're not trading enough. These hidden costs can add up. And remember that you can always ask your broker for a discount—especially if you're a good customer.

ONLINE BROKERS

WE COME AGAIN TO THE INTERNET. AS IT HAS WITH MANY industries, the Internet is turning the commission-brokerage industry upside down.

If you feel comfortable making your own investment decisions (as you must if you use a discount broker), you can point and click and pay less for investing than at any time in history. Internet brokers such as Ameritrade, E*Trade, DLJDirect, Waterhouse Securities, Muriel Siebert, and others charge low commissions, in the neighborhood of $8 or $10 a trade. And it's not just upstart online brokers who are in this business. Established discount and full-service brokers have seen the future and realize that it involves the Internet. In addition to low commissions, these outfits are offering top-notch financial information on their Web sites.

The unfortunate thing about Internet trading is that it sometimes tempts investors to trade more than is wise. It seems you can't pick up a newspaper anymore without reading about day traders, who have given up their jobs to sit home and click away, investing via the Internet. "Short term" doesn't begin to describe their investing horizon: they hold positions for a few hours or even minutes. Despite the publicity day traders have received, studies show that the majority of them lose money. So the trick to being a good individual investor on the Internet is the same as for investing the traditional way: develop the discipline to research, buy, and hold stocks for the long term.

The other problems that many Internet investors have reported are technical ones. Typical complaints: trades not being executed in a timely fashion and investors not being able to get through on the Web sites they use.

Several of the personal finance magazines, including *SmartMoney* and *Kiplinger's,* have run excellent surveys of online brokers, and Gomez Advisors (**www.gomez.com**) tracks the performance of online brokers. Take a look at current rankings before signing up with an online broker.

BUYING STOCK WITHOUT A MIDDLEMAN

ONE PROBLEM WITH BUYING STOCKS THROUGH A BROKER, especially if you're just starting out and are only buying a few shares, is that there may be a minimum commission. If a brokerage firm's minimum commission is $50 and you want to buy ten shares of stock at $40 a share, your commission is a hefty 12 percent of your investment. If you're starting out small, these minimums can make a stock purchase a spectacularly bad buy. Sometimes they can even cost more than the stock itself. But once again, Wall Street proves itself flexible. There are a couple of different avenues you can pursue if you want to buy stock without going through a broker at all.

For decades, investors have bought stock without paying commissions through **dividend reinvestment plans (DRIPs)**. We talked about these in Chapter 2. If you have a DRIP and a company issues a dividend, instead of getting a check in the mail you automatically get more stock in the company. When you own stock, you should always sign up for DRIPs. But a problem arises. To enroll you need to already own at least a share of stock. So how do you buy your first shares without paying commissions? There are ways.

For one thing, some companies allow you to buy stock directly from them—about 350 companies and mutual funds participate in the Direct Stock Purchase Plan Clearinghouse (**www.enrolldirect.com**). The Web site has information on the stocks you can buy, which include McDonald's and Mattel.

The National Association of Investors Corp. (NAIC) has a low-cost investment plan that allows you to buy stock in more than 150 firms for a small fee (the cost of the stock plus $7 per company and a $10 fee to cover any stock price fluctuations). More info on this plan can be found at NAIC's Web site: **www.better-investing.org**. Two other avenues for buying stock are worth noting. First Share is a membership organization that allows you to buy stock from other members. It costs $18 to join, and stock purchases cost $12, plus the price of the stock. For more information, call 800-683-0743. And *Moneypaper* is a newsletter (subscription is $81 a year) that buys shares of more than 1,000 companies. The cost per trade is $20, plus the market price of the stock. For information on *Moneypaper*, call 800-388-9993. Another source of information on commission-free investing is a book, *Buying Stocks Without a Broker*, by Charles B. Carlson (McGraw Hill, 1992, $17.95). (See "Kinds of Stock Orders" on the following page.)

Kinds of Stock Orders

BACK TO YOUR FOREIGN LANGUAGE vocabulary lessons. Below are the types of orders you can place when you're buying or selling stocks.

>>**Market order.** You want to buy or sell shares now, at the best price available. "I want 100 shares of Microsoft today at market price."

>>**Limit order.** You want to buy or sell stock, but only if certain prices are available. "I want to buy 100 shares of Microsoft at 95 or better" means if the price is above 95, your order won't be executed. Another example of a limit order: "Sell my Microsoft shares when the price goes up to 100 or above."

>>**Stop-loss order.** You want to sell your stock if it drops to a certain level to protect yourself against bigger losses. "Sell my Microsoft stock if it gets down to 85 or below."
Be careful to specify that you want it sold if it hits a certain

TAXES AND MORE TAXES

WE NOW TURN TO THE UNPLEASANT TOPIC OF TAXES. YOU owe taxes on the money you make, whether you make it by flipping burgers at a fast-food joint or by profitably investing your little nest egg. The Internal Revenue Service gets a cut either way.

There are two kinds of income: earned (from a job) and unearned (from investment or interest income.) A savings account or stock brokerage account generates interest income.

level "or below." If you just specify a particular price, it's possible that the trading will skip your price on its way down and you'll be left holding a stock you wanted to get rid of. Example: If you want to sell XYZ stock if it gets down to 50 and trading skips from 52 to 49, your sell order won't be executed unless you've made it clear that you want to sell at 50 or below.

When you place an order, remember to state how long it's good for. Do you want this order to be executed today only? Do you want the order to stand until it's canceled or executed?

>>**Round Lots and Odd Lots.** Stock orders are generally given in round lots—that is, groups of 100. An odd lot is an order that is not in hundreds—57 shares, for instance, or 161 shares. Odd lots generally cost more to trade than round lots.

>>**Bid, Ask, and Spread.** The spread is the difference between the bid (the price someone is offering to buy for) and the ask (the price someone is willing to sell for).

Earned Income

IF YOU'RE A DEPENDENT (OF YOUR PARENTS, FOR EXAMPLE), single, and under age sixty-five and you earn less than $4,300, you don't have to file a tax return. (That figure was for a 1999 tax return, and it changes frequently. Check the IRS Web site, **www.irs.gov**, for the latest figure.) However, you might want to file anyway, because you may have had income tax withheld from your paychecks and therefore be due a refund.

Unearned Income

IF YOU'RE UNDER THE AGE OF FOURTEEN AND YOU EARNED less than $700 in investment income in 1999, you don't have to file your own tax return.

If you're under the age of fourteen and you earned between $700 and $7,000 in investment income (and *only* from interest and investment income), your parents can usually include you on their income tax return, although you may want to file your own. (If you file your own return, you may be able to take certain tax deductions that you couldn't otherwise take.)

The first $700 of the income isn't taxable, and the next $700 is taxed at the child's rate, which is usually 15 percent. If the child's investment income is more than $1,400, anything over that is taxed at the parents' rate. (This is why having a lot of money in a custodial account doesn't make sense for your parents.)

If you're a kid over the age of fourteen and a dependent of your parents, you don't have to file a tax return if your only investment income is under $700. If it's more than that, you have to file your own tax return—you can't be included on your parents'. All of your investment income is taxed at your rate—not your parents' rate. Your tax rate is probably 15 percent (unless you're a child who happens to be a highly paid movie star).

IT GOES WITHOUT SAYING THAT AN ENTIRE BOOK COULD BE written about taxes. In fact, several excellent ones have been, and for more detail I would recommend consulting one. *JK Lasser's Your Income Tax* and *The Ernst & Young Tax Guide* are two valuable resources that are updated yearly. In addition, the IRA has—believe it or not—a helpful Web site, at **www.irs.gov**. (Although be warned about tax Web sites: this is one area where books still reign. I took a look at one tax site and noticed that printing the file would have required 150 pages!)

ROTH IRAS

PROBABLY THE LAST THING YOU ARE INTERESTED IN HEARING about is retirement. When you haven't even begun your career yet, it's tough to see your way to the end of it. But I want to briefly touch on Roth IRAs. They are a way to start saving for retirement, and they are a spectacular idea. You already know the power of letting money earn compound interest for a long period of time. A Roth IRA is built for such a goal.

You are eligible to start a Roth as soon as you have earned income (not investment income). You can make a yearly contribution of up to $2,000 (nondeductible) provided you aren't making more than $95,000 a year (for single individuals). Your contribution can't amount to more than your earnings, so if you made $1,000 last year, that's the most you could contribute. If you need a graphic illustration of why you should start a Roth IRA as soon as you have earned income, consult the table below. It will show you the startling advantage you can gain by starting to save and invest early. (See "Who Wants to Be a Millionaire?" on pages 84–85.)

In a Roth IRA your earnings grow tax-free. When it comes time to withdraw money, you may be able to do that tax-free, too, depending on the circumstances.

One reason young people often hesitate to contribute to an IRA is because it ties up your money for a long time. What if you want to use the money to buy your first house when you're thirty? Under old IRA regulations, if you withdraw the money before you're a certain age, there can be penalties.

But with a Roth IRA you can always withdraw the money you put in, without penalty. (Remember, you don't get a tax deduction for Roth contributions.) And you can withdraw earnings on your contributions after the Roth IRA is five years old without any penalty if you meet certain requirements. For your purpos-

Who Wants to Be a Millionaire?

WITH ALL DUE APOLOGIES TO REGIS PHILBIN, we know a more reliable way to become a millionaire than to appear on a quiz show. The chart at right shows how much you would need to invest each month, based on your age, to retire at 65 with $1 million. The second column assumes a return on investment of 8 percent per year. That's a conservative, reasonable return. The third column assumes a return of 11 percent per year, which is what the stock market has averaged over the past 70 years. The fourth column is how much you'd need to invest if you were to do better than the historical averages and make 15 percent per year.

This table illustrates what a dramatic difference a little time makes. As you can see, if you started investing when you were 15, you'd need a little more than $7 a month (at 15 percent gain); if you waited until you were 30 years old, you'd need nearly ten times that much each month. Although many teens think they should wait until they can "afford" to invest, this table makes clear the high cost of waiting.

es, one of the most interesting of these requirements is if you're using the money to buy a first home: in that case you can withdraw up to $10,000 of Roth IRA earnings tax-free. If you wait until you're older than fifty-nine and a half, you can withdraw earnings tax-free in any case.

The bottom line: the Roth IRA is a great idea. If you have earned income and can set one up, do it. Maybe your parents would even be willing to help out for such a worthy cause. If you made $1,000 last summer, for example, you could put the entire amount into a Roth IRA, where it will sit and earn com-

This method takes time, and achieving millionaire status doesn't happen as quickly as with a lottery or game show. But on the other hand, this is a sure-fire way to become a millionaire, not a long shot. (Note the chart doesn't take taxes into account.)

AGE	8%: $/MONTH	11%: $/MONTH	15%: $/MONTH
8	$71.57	$17.88	$2.55
10	$84.10	$22.27	$3.44
12	$98.86	$27.74	$4.63
15	$126.08	$38.57	$7.25
18	$160.97	$53.66	$11.34
20	$189.59	$66.90	$15.28
25	$286.45	$116.28	$32.24
30	$435.94	$202.91	$68.13
35	$670.98	$356.57	$144.44
40	$1,051.50	$634.46	$308.31
45	$1,697.73	$1,155.22	$667.90
50	$2,889.85	$2,199.30	$1,495.87

SOURCE: BLOOMBERG LP

pounded investment returns for thirty or forty years and your parents could reimburse you.

How should you invest your Roth IRA? With an eye to the long term, obviously. There are no special rules on investing an IRA—you can put it into mutual funds or stocks, although it must be in a formal Roth IRA account to comply with various regulations. Tuck it away to grow, and know that you've made an incredibly smart move.

If You Have $1,000 to Invest

IF YOU WANTED TO START INVESTING and had $1,000, where should you begin?

We queried several well-respected and thoughtful pros on what advice they'd give to a young investor just starting out.

"Assuming you had earned income and were eligible to put it in a Roth IRA, that's what I'd do. I'd invest the Roth in an index fund, like Vanguard's Total Market index fund. It gives you exposure to large- and small-cap companies, and has low expenses. It's kind of a no-brainer, and not as exciting as buying the latest XYZ.com stock, but that's what I'd do."

> STEWART WELCH III, the Welch Group, one of
> *Worth Magazine*'s Top 300 Financial Advisers
> in America, minimum client account: $1 million

"I'd put the money in a mutual fund; obviously I'm predisposed to think that way. I'd put it in a fund that specializes in buying stocks with low P/Es—a value fund."

> JOHN NEFF, retired manager of the Windsor Fund
> and senior vice president of Wellington
> Management Company

"With $1,000 to invest, I'd hate to see a kid lose the money, especially just starting out, so I would tell them to put it in a mutual fund. If they had a real interest in stocks, put half in a mutual fund and with the other half, research a stock and buy it."

> ANDREW DAVIS, manager of Davis Convertible
> Securities and Davis Real Estate funds

MAKING MOM OR DAD
YOUR PARTNER

CHANCES ARE, YOUR PARENTS ARE MIGHTY PLEASED THAT you're interested in investing and the stock market. From their point of view, the fact that you're paying attention to the stock market at all shows promise. It's a real-live sign of maturity; after all, there are lots of thirty-year-olds who don't have a clue about investments. It also raises parental hopes that you will be self-supporting and financially independent someday. Intellectually they know that, but seeing you scanning the stock pages of the newspaper or logging on to an Internet site to check your investments warms the hearts of parents everywhere. While most parents would tell their kids—truthfully—that money doesn't buy happiness, I don't know of any parents who don't wish prosperity on their kids. And let's face it, investing may give you some common ground with your parents—you may not be able to converse with them about new trends in music, but the two of you can always marvel together at how high the technology stocks are trading.

So if the folks are so tickled that you have a mind for money, why not conspire to make your parents your partner in investing? Plenty of parents—and grandparents—have staked kids in their investing, figuring that even if they lose the money, it's such a valuable lesson it's worth it. Here are a couple of the ways families have worked things out.

Jon and Matt Wickert of Newark, Delaware, became investing partners with their father, Alan, when they were seventeen and fourteen. Alan Wickert, like many parents, had set up savings accounts for his sons when they were young. When Jon and Matt hit their teens, their dad decided that the accounts, which by then had about $1,700 each in them, were theirs to invest. They opened custodial accounts with a discount broker that had

Beware of the Cold Call

ONE OF MY FAVORITE business cartoons, which I have pinned to the bulletin board in my office, appeared in *The Wall Street Journal*. It shows a man talking on the telephone, saying, "But I'll certainly keep you in mind in case I ever take leave of my senses and decide to entrust all my savings to a complete stranger on the phone."

That man was fielding a cold call. The one downside to becoming a successful investor is that it sets you up for the dreaded cold calls from brokers who want you to do business with them.

Many of the calls are from well-meaning brokers who may be just starting out or looking to build their business. They've taken your name off some mailing or telemarketing list—or maybe just out of the phone book. These calls can be an annoyance, but the brokers usually are polite when you tell them you're not interested. As a minor, you might want to remind them that you can't legally buy or sell stocks.

But the dangerous calls are the high-pressure pitches from disreputable brokers who are pushing junk stocks. These guys are often reading from a script (firms sometimes employ out-of-work actors to make initial calls), and included in the script are comeback lines for every objection you might raise.

If you're an active investor when you hit adulthood, you may well receive this type of call. It helps to become educated about their lines so that you can recognize a pitch when you

online computer trading capabilities. Jon and Matt had the final say on what stocks to buy, and their father promised he'd give advice only when he was asked. The two bought stocks like Nike, Xerox, Bell Atlantic, General Electric, and Netscape and hear one. They may start with a phrase like "Are you interested in making money?" Remember, no one can guarantee you an investment return. They will try to get you to divulge details about your personal financial situation to feel you out about how much you have to spend. (They want to know how much to try to sell you.) Don't talk about your personal finances over the phone with any strangers.

If you tell them you want to talk things over with your parents—or someone else, like an adviser or trusted friend—they'll try to embarrass you out of doing so with a line like "Come on, are you going to ask your parents for permission forever?" "I thought you were an adult now," or "Do you depend on other people to make your decisions?" Don't be intimidated; the wisest investors often bounce ideas off advisers.

They may try to put you under time pressure to make a decision, telling you about an offer that expires or saying they have a limited amount of the stock to sell. This is an old sales tactic; tell them that you don't appreciate or respond to that type of pressure.

If you're on the receiving end of any of these tactics, simply tell the caller you're not interested, that you're hanging up the phone, and then do it. If you have a complaint about a cold caller, you can contact the North American Securities Administration Association (NASAA) toll free at 888-84-NASAA.

are avid followers of the market. Matt was interested enough and did well enough with his account that his father then let him manage his own $33,000 IRA account at a discount broker. Although he set up guidelines for that account (a certain per-

Can You Spare $20 a Month?

WHAT WILL $20 A MONTH BUY? A new CD? A large pizza with toppings and a round of soft drinks for you and a few friends?

It could buy you a very nice nest egg. Twenty dollars a month isn't all that much. If you're a teenager with an active babysitting or lawn mowing business, you're probably making more than that each month. If you started faithfully investing that amount you'd barely miss it, and before long your investment would begin to add up. Once you're an adult and earning a full-time income, $20 a month would make an even smaller dent in your wallet.

Below you can see what $20 invested month after month after month will add up to after a number of years. I've assumed an annual rate of 10 percent, which is actually below historical stock market returns. So what are you waiting for?

$20 A MONTH INVESTED	WOULD GROW TO
After ten years	$3,997.28
After twenty years	$14,365.18
After thirty years	$41,256.87
After forty years	$111,006.96
After fifty years	$291,920.75

SOURCE: BLOOMBERG LP

centage had to be in mutual funds), he again gave his son free rein to choose the investments.

Chris Davis's father took a different tack. Shelby Davis, the chief executive officer of mutual fund advisers Davis Selected Advisers, didn't want his children to be afraid of losing money in the market, and so he offered them an incentive to buy stock.

He told them that if they had good reasons for investing in a particular stock and it went down, he'd cover their losses. Now that's not something that happens in real life, of course, but it helped Chris and his brother and sister be willing to take some risks. "You had to have a well-reasoned argument for buying a stock, but he backed you up once you did," says Chris, who is now thirty-four and a money manager himself. "It's like teaching a kid to be a circus performer. You first take him up on the high wire with a harness to protect him while he's learning. When he's learned, you let him go without it."

And many a parent and grandparent can simply buy a gift of stock for a birthday or holiday, instead of spending the same amount of money on clothes you'll never wear. Drop some hints. If your grandparents are the type who buy you savings bonds, mention stocks or mutual funds that you have researched as an alternative to the savings bonds. They'll get the hint.

"The difference between getting somewhere and getting nowhere is the courage to make an early start."

CHARLES M. SCHWAB

"I Remember My First Stock"

THE TITANS OF THE INVESTMENT WORLD WERE ALL young once. They, too, had to deal with high school, acne, and that seemingly endless wait to get a driver's license.

Not surprisingly, like you, many of them showed a precocious interest in the stock market. In addition to tackling all the normal challenges of being a teen and young adult, they found themselves poring over newspaper stock tables and even putting their money where their convictions were. Legendary investor Warren Buffett (who often comes in second after Bill Gates on the *Forbes* 400 Rich List and was worth, as of 1999, an estimated $31 billion) was reading investment books at age twelve and shorting AT&T by the time he was a high school senior, according to biographer Roger Lowenstein in *Buffett: The Making of an American Capitalist*. Michael Price, who managed the Mutual Shares funds and routinely produced annual returns of 20 percent before selling the fund company to another firm, saw the first stock he ever bought—while in junior high—triple in value.

We interviewed some of Wall Street's brightest and found there were useful lessons to be learned from their growing pains. All had some successful stock picks early on, but they also saw some of their stocks go sour—and, as always, in some ways it was the investment failures that taught them the most. You can profit from their experiences.

JAMES J. CRAMER

"JUST LIKE YOU WANT YOUR TEAM TO WIN, I WANTED MY STOCKS TO WIN."

JAMES J. CRAMER IS A STOCK MARKET TRADER FOR THE electronic age. As president of the New York-based Cramer, Berkowitz & Co., he manages money for wealthy investors. As a founder, cochairman and daily columnist of TheStreet.com (**www.thestreet.com**), the lively and engaging financial news site, and as a regular on TheStreet.com's weekly show on Fox TV, he gives investors his informed and refreshingly opinionated insights into the market.

Not surprisingly, the stock market has long been a passion of Cramer's, and he credits his businessman father with sparking his initial interest. "My father taught me about the market. He had a brilliant idea. He said everyone is going to read the sports section of the newspaper, but the business section can be just as interesting," says Cramer. "He had me pick stocks and try to figure out which ones were going to go up and which ones were going down. He presented it as a tremendous amusement."

Soon the second-grader was keeping a ledger of the stocks he followed. "My dad would stay late at work to bring home the late edition of the *Philadelphia Bulletin,* which had the closing stock prices for the day."

But the whole enterprise was less about real cash than it was about pinpointing winning stocks. "Just like you want your team to win, I wanted my stocks to win," says Cramer. "We had two board games—one was called *Stocks and Bonds* and the other was called *Acquire*—and I played them until I wore them out. I also developed my own stock market game in fifth grade, which I showed to my class."

Cramer's fascination with the market wasn't a passing interest; he remained enthralled through college, Harvard Law school, and his first two careers, as a journalist and as a stockbroker for Goldman Sachs in New York.

Although he was a market junkie from a young age, Cramer didn't start actually investing until he was out of college and had money to put into the market in the early 1980s. (He's not counting the five shares of Continental Bank he was given as a bar mitzvah gift by his grandfather, a holding he has clung to through a couple of mergers.) The first stock he bought? American Agronomics, which he learned about in a *Forbes* article. "It went from 7 to 9, then got wiped out by frost. I held on, and it finally merged and I did OK, but it taught me a lesson. It was cheap, and there was a reason; there was this weather variable," he says with a laugh.

Other early investments: SPS Technologies, went up 20 points after he bought it ("It made fasteners for airplanes and caught a defense cycle"), and Natomas, an oil company, was acquired by Diamond Shamrock soon after he bought the stock. Early stumbles included the women's clothing company Bobbie Brooks. "Again, I bought it off a *Forbes* article," says Cramer. "The article said it could be on a comeback. It wasn't."

He soon moved into trading options and made money by betting heavily against airline companies. He bought puts, a strategy for making money when a stock is dropping in price (see page 61). "I thought, 'People's Express [a now-defunct no-frills airline] sucks, so I'll bet against them,'" he says. When he started law school, he would leave stock tips on his telephone answering machine, check prices, and make trades between classes. One day he had a meeting at a Cambridge, Massachusetts, coffee shop with an editor of a magazine he wrote for. The editor told him he'd made money off Cramer's telephone answering machine stock picks, handed him a check for $500,000, and asked Cramer to invest it for him. Thus was a money manager born.

But despite Cramer's status today as a full-time, professional money manager, he is an advocate of what he calls "the Home Depot school" of personal finance: do it yourself. "A model has developed in this country of handing it off to others, which has become expensive, very inefficient, and not trustworthy," he says. "It's like Home Depot. You figure it out. There are some jobs you can't do yourself, but most jobs you can. If you have no knowledge of it, you get ripped off."

He is dazzled by the resources available to kids today ("The Web is just unbelievable") and muses on how the landscape of Wall Street has changed since he was in school. "My father always thought that investing was an insider's game, and I think that view was somewhat justified a couple of decades ago. But it's not like 1963 anymore. The club has been opened up, and investing has become a people's game now."

ALEXANDRA LEBENTHAL

"MUTUAL FUNDS ARE THE WAY TO GO FOR ME."

AS A CHILD, ALEXANDRA LEBENTHAL'S INVESTMENT EDUCA-tion centered not on stocks but on bonds. That's not surprising, considering that her grandparents began the Wall Street bond brokerage firm, Lebenthal & Co. back in 1925, and her father, Jim Lebenthal, ran the firm for years before turning over the reins to Alexandra. (He still serves as the firm's chairman, while Alexandra is president and chief executive.)

During school vacations, Alexandra often helped out her strong-willed grandmother, Sayra Lebenthal, in the office. While her grandmother instilled in her the basics of running a business and taking care of customers, her father made sure she understood bonds and what bond financing could accomplish. "I remember my father taking us to the World Trade Center to watch it being built and talking to us about how they got the money to build it." When Alexandra and her brother and sister received financial gifts from her grandmother, they were bonds, not stocks. "We always used to wish she'd give us cash instead," laughs Lebenthal.

It all added up to a thorough education in business and in bonds, but not necessarily in the stock market. It was when she graduated from Princeton University that her education in equities began. "I gravitated to Wall Street, like everyone else in the mid 1980s," she says, "and went to work at Kidder Peabody." At the age of twenty-three, with her first bonus check for $5,000 from Kidder Peabody in her pocket, she made her first individual investment: some New York City tax-free municipal bonds, and 100 shares of Jaguar, the auto company. "Jaguar was one of the stupidest investments I have ever made. Looking back, I don't really know why I made that investment—perhaps because I thought it was a good product or something like that. It went down about 30 percent before I sold it," she says.

Over the next several years, Lebenthal gained ground in both her business career and her investment portfolio. She left Kidder Peabody and went to work at the family firm, serving an apprenticeship with her ninety-one-year-old grandmother, and taking over her grandmother's client accounts. A few years later she took over as president of Lebenthal & Co.

Meanwhile, she was continuing to invest. By both temperament and training, Alexandra Lebenthal is a conservative investor who conscientiously salts money away regularly. "In the

What is Bill Gates Worth? ...Or Warren Buffett? ...Or Larry Ellison?

EVERYONE HAS HEARD OF BILL GATES. He's the cofounder of Microsoft, who has been at or near the top of the lists of the richest people in America for the last fifteen years or so. Warren Buffett, who runs Berkshire Hathaway and has become the most famous investor of our time ($10,000 invested with Buffett in 1965 is now worth $51 million), has occasionally topped his friend Gates in the *Forbes* 400 Rich List. And Larry Ellison, who founded Oracle, arguably the world's leading data-base software company, is fabulously wealthy, too. He's been near the top of the lists, although he has never made it as "King of the Hill." For example, in last year's *Forbes* Rich List Gates was number one with $85 billion, Buffett ranked number three with $31 billion, and Ellison was a not-too-shabby number twelve with $13 billion.

But last spring newspaper reports were crowning Ellison as having topped Gates in the net worth department. How could that have happened in what was a relatively short period of time?

The answer sheds some light on how the people who create such lists get these numbers. The biggest share of an investor's wealth usually comes from the value of the stock they own in their companies. The listmakers multiply the number of shares of Microsoft stock that Gates owns by the stock price on any given day. Not surprisingly, if the stock price of Microsoft, or any company, rises or falls dramatically so does the net worth figure of the mogul. And as we know, stocks go up and down all the time.

ant and the grasshopper story (where the ant painstakingly prepares for the future and the grasshopper doesn't), I'm a typical ant. I put money away and invest regularly," she says.

What accounted for most of the rise in Ellison's net worth and the drop in Gates's last spring was the fact that Microsoft stock went down and Oracle stock went up. By the time you read this, Ellison may have dropped back down on the list, or seen an even greater rise in his net worth figure.

It's useful to remember when you hear that someone like Bill Gates, Warren Buffett, or Larry Ellison is worth a ba-zillion dollars that they don't have that much cash sitting around in the bank. In fact, you can bet that if they did try to cash in all of their stock, investors everywhere would see it as a sign that they, too, should sell. The result would be that the stock price would drop through the basement and Gates, Buffett, or Ellison couldn't get anywhere near $50 billion, or whatever the current value of their stock is. Of course, you don't have to waste any worry or sympathy on these guys. It's safe to say that they're financially fixed for life—but the exact size of their fortune is at the mercy of the stock market.

While you're at it, if you're going to idolize Gates or Buffett or Ellison, perhaps the size of his bankbook isn't what is worth admiring. Each has, in his own way, made an impact by revolutionizing a part of a business. I'd hate to think that the "worth" of a person could be measured by a dollar figure. So maybe if the answer to the question is a dollar amount, like $50 billion, the right question isn't "What is he worth?" but, "How much are his financial assets worth at this moment?"

In individual stocks, Apple Computer was a big winner for her: she bought it at 13 and sold it at 100. She bought another stock, E-Tek Dynamics, a fiber optics manufacturer, at 28 and sold it about ten or eleven months later for 100. She was delighted with that return until a few weeks later, when the company was announced it was being acquired and the stock shot up past 280. She bought, and still holds, stock in Charles Schwab, which has risen nicely while she has owned it.

But along the way, Alexandra Lebenthal was coming to a realization about her investing style. "I realized that I am not a good investor in individual stocks. I get way too emotionally tied up in the ups and downs of the market," she says.

Ironically it wasn't a losing stock that finally made her decide that individual stocks were not her strength, but a winner. "I had a wild ride with Amazon, and that is what sealed my distaste for individual stocks," says Lebenthal. "I bought it in the winter of 1999 and held on to it; I could have sold after about two weeks for a substantial profit, but I was greedy and didn't." During that winter and spring Amazon was wildly volatile, and swung back below where Alexandra had purchased it. "It went back up again and I finally sold out at what was almost Amazon's all-time high, but there wasn't a lot of satisfaction in it," she says. She found herself arriving at the office and being preoccupied, checking the stock several times a day. She decided that the distraction wasn't worth it. "I feel much more comfortable investing in mutual funds. I periodically look where they are; I see they've been going up and I don't get tied up in the daily ups and downs." So, while she still holds some stocks, she's more inclined now to invest via funds. One strategy she does employ with her individual stocks is using them to make charitable donations. "When I have a big gain in a stock, lots of times I use the stock to make a charitable donation so I don't have to pay the capital gains tax," she says, pointing to a strategy any investor can use. (An investor who has a stock that goes from $10 to $20 a share pays tax on the increase. But an investor who donates that stock to a charity gets a tax deduction for the market value, and escapes the tax.)

Mutual funds have not only given Lebenthal the ability to sleep better, and to ignore the stock market ticker at work, but they have given her better performance, too. "While I have had some home runs in stocks, I have had more things that went down a lot," she says candidly.

"Particularly in sectors like technology, mutual funds are the way to go for me," she says. "Everyone wants the company that is going to hit the ball out of the park, but there are a lot that don't do well. I own Goldman Sachs Internet Tollkeeper Fund, which at this moment is up 109 percent in the last four months. I'm participating in all these companies that have been going up every day but I don't have to be the one to pull the trigger and say buy or sell."

As might be expected, Lebenthal does hold bonds as well. "I probably have more bonds in my portfolio than someone my age would normally have," she says. "I also have bond funds, so I'm getting some growth and compounding there, and I have closed end bond funds which I bought at a discount. I'm looking for appreciation there as well," she says. But for teenage investors, she suggests sticking to stocks. "If a teenager had $1,000 to invest, I'd recommend a stock mutual fund. Depending on how comfortable they were with the market moving up and down and with risk, I'd say that would determine how aggressive a fund they should go into. On the face of it, you can say that a sixteen year old should be in an aggressive fund, but if the market goes down it could be detrimental to their long term psyche."

> **>STREET SLANG**
> **INSIDER TRADING**
> **Profiting from access to important information about a company that isn't public knowledge** (for example, if the firm you work for is secretly planning to acquire another company). **This is illegal.** Those who engage in insider trading often wear Wall Street's most embarrassing fashion accessory: handcuffs.

Does the idea of a Wall Street pro turning her investing over to a mutual fund manager cause any embarrassment to her? "Absolutely not," she says. "Even though I am a sophisticated investor and a professional I'm not a portfolio manager. I could have been and probably would have been good at it, but that's not what the head of Goldman Sachs or Merrill Lynch or any of those firms does. They have people who pick stocks. When it comes down to it, we're all individual investors."

JOHN NEFF

"SOMEHOW I GOT HOLD OF A PAMPHLET ON THE STOCK MARKET AND READ IT."

DURING THE MORE THAN THREE DECADES THAT JOHN NEFF managed Vanguard Windsor Fund, he racked up a record that was the envy of Wall Street. These days—when it seems as if the performance of mutual fund managers gets measured in months, not years, and this year's star investor can be next semester's has-been—Neff's performance is all the more noteworthy. He beat the market for twenty-two of the thirty-one years he managed Windsor. His average annual return over the five years ending October 31, 1995, when he retired, was 20.5 percent a year (versus the S&P 500's 17.2 percent). Over his entire tenure at the fund, his average annual return was 13.7 percent, compared with the S&P 500's 10.6 percent. To put it in numbers we can all appreciate, if you'd invested $10,000 with him in 1964 when he started, you'd have had $564,637 (assuming you reinvested all dividends and capital gains) by the time he turned over the reins to the next manager. Neff accomplished this by being a value investor—consistently finding unappreciated, undervalued stocks, buying them, and holding them until their price made a comeback.

So if Neff made his mark in investing by taking the unconventional route, it's fitting that his introduction to the stock market involved a less-traveled path, too.

Although he had some exposure to the market as a youngster, he didn't dive in immediately. "When I was in sixth grade, we studied Alaska and the stock market in school as special projects," says Neff. "Studying stocks was unusual, especially then; this was around 1940. I was very interested, but I did nothing more with investing at that time. I've read that Warren Buffett owned stocks from sixth grade on; I didn't have the money, and I just didn't pursue it. Of course in the 1940s we had other distractions; World War II was going on." So, as he says, "The seed that was planted was dormant for quite a time." Rather than going right to college after high school, Neff went to work, first as a shipping clerk for a jukebox manufacturer and then for his father's company, before volunteering for the Navy during the Korean War. "I had been in the naval reserve in high school, and I was draft age, so I volunteered for twenty-four months of active duty," he says. His father made Neff an offer. "He told me if I bought stock in Aro Equipment, he would guarantee me against any loss." Aro, a company started by Neff's great-uncle, made lubrication equipment for garages and gas stations and was traded on the American Stock Exchange. "Even I knew that was a good offer," he says.

He spent much of his military service in Jacksonville, Florida, and Norfolk, Virginia, helping to maintain Navy jets. "I did a lot of detail work in the Navy," he says, "and I lollygagged around a lot. Somehow I got hold of a pamphlet on the stock market and read it. I read about common and preferred stock, but I knew so little about it in those days, I had to write and ask my father which type I owned in Aro, common or preferred. It was common stock." Neff's father never had to make good on his offer to cover his son's losses in Aro. Neff sold the stock after "two or three" years and doubled his money.

When Neff got out of the Navy, he finished his college degree in two years. It was at the University of Toledo that Neff's interest in the market was ignited by a finance professor, Sidney Robbins. "I only took a couple of finance courses, but I really got roped in," says Neff. He started out as an analyst for a Cleveland bank, newly married and determined to grow his own portfolio. "I had $1,000 or $1,500 that I turned into $3,000," he says. "We were just married, and there were any number of things we could have used that for, but we didn't spend it. We hung on."

Although Neff mostly stuck to investing in common stocks, he did use one strategy to leverage his capital. "I bought convertible bonds on margin," he says. "It's the intelligent way to use margin. I'd tippy-toe to the Cleveland Trust (which, besides his then-employer, National Bank of Cleveland, was the other big bank in town) and borrow to buy convertible bonds. There's not a lot of downside to them. The **coupon** (meaning the interest payments you receive on the convertible bond) can carry the loan."

Neff's advice to young investors comes from a lifetime of sensible value investing: "Save some money and invest, but do it prudently and wisely." With the Dow at about 10,500 in 1999 as he made these recommendations, Neff the contrarian couldn't resist suggesting that the market is overpriced for bargain hunters. "Be aware that maybe now isn't the best time to be fully invested in stocks," he says.

JONATHAN STEINBERG

"IF I COULD INVEST IN ANYTHING,
IS THIS WHAT I WOULD INVEST IN?
THE STUFF THAT'S IN MY PORTFOLIO NOW?"

"I WAS THIRTEEN WHEN I BOUGHT MY FIRST STOCK," SAYS Jonathan Steinberg, founder, chairman, and chief executive officer of Individual Investor Group, which publishes *Individual*

Investor magazine. "I took $1,000 of my bar mitzvah money and invested in Abbott Laboratories. I made about a 30 percent return. It was a positive experience, which is nice for your first time out."

Steinberg, thirty-four, had a natural interest in business. He also gained investment celebrity as a six-time winner of *The Wall Street Journal's* Dartboard stock-picking competition, in which professional investors stack their portfolios against one of randomly chosen stocks—the "Dartboard" refers to the idea of throwing darts at a stock page and buying whichever stocks the darts lands on. "I understood early that business meant all goods and services. Entertainment can be business, and sports can be business; everything can be business. And it can be very exciting," he says.

His interest drove him to throw himself into reading the business press. "From the age of thirteen, I was reading *The Wall Street Journal* every day plus several business magazines, and shortly thereafter I subscribed to *Value Line*. A lot of learning about investing is getting comfortable with the terminology. If you read *The Wall Street Journal* every day for a few years, you'll pick it up."

He also made use of some high-powered business expertise that was at his disposal. "I learned a lot talking to my dad and asking other people about investing. You can't be afraid to ask questions," he says. Jonathan Steinberg had a high-profile role model in his father, financier Saul Steinberg, former chairman of Reliance Group Holdings, Inc., an insurance holding company. "My dad told me—with great conviction—that if I wanted to know a stock as well as anyone in the world, all I had to do was do the work. The information was there and publicly available. I had an inherent confidence that I could do this."

But investing is more than research and theory; Steinberg strongly believes that there's no substitute for hands-on experience. "You have to go out and do it. I highly recommend the trading games, which we didn't have back when I was starting out. They can be very constructive, and it's a nice way to experiment with different trading strategies."

Steinberg continued his own tutorial, practicing not only buying stocks but also such strategies as short selling. "I made a conscious effort to try to be a connoisseur of investing. I sold Western Union short. I did that solely off reading *Value Line*," he says. "I saw that capital expenditures exceeded cash flow for many years and that Western Union's balance sheet was getting weaker and weaker. I thought there would be a change in perception of their business, and I got lucky and it happened quickly. The stock just collapsed." Steinberg is quick to say that he doesn't think teens should routinely short stocks. "It has greater risk, and it's hard. There can be emotional components and real financial pressures if a stock you've shorted starts to go up." (Steinberg is referring to the panic an investor can feel when a stock they've gambled on to decline in price starts to go up instead. Theoretically, there's almost no limit to your losses.)

Looking back, Steinberg thinks his biggest investment mistakes as a young investor came when he failed to diversify his portfolio. "I was concentrated too much in one area. At one time I was too concentrated in Massey Ferguson stock, a farming equipment company. I was trying for a big score and not being disciplined enough."

He did develop a few strategies that he likes to pass along to new investors. The first involves knowing when to sell a stock. "I always tell people that if a stock is doing really well, it's never a mistake to take out the cost of the security. You've taken out the money you invested in it, and then you can relax and let the winners run." Another involves a method he used to jump-start his portfolio if he felt it wasn't performing well: sell everything. "That way I had a clean slate and could start fresh. I wasn't encumbered by emotional ties, and I could ask myself: If I could invest in anything, is this what I would invest in? The stuff that's in my portfolio now?"

These days, since Steinberg's company publishes an investing magazine, he doesn't actively invest. Instead all his personal investments are in mutual funds. That's to prevent even the appearance of a conflict of interest, which could come if the magazine wrote about stocks that he owned and it looked as if he were trying to hype his own stocks. "I'm committed to the magazine, and I can't invest in individual stocks," he says. "But I'll admit it's tempting sometimes."

ANDREW DAVIS AND CHRIS DAVIS

"WOULD YOU WANT TO OWN THE ENTIRE COMPANY?"

TEENAGERS WHO HAVE DAYDREAMED, EVEN BRIEFLY, ABOUT what life would be like without annoying siblings and parents might be astonished to hear of brothers who have chosen to work together—in the family investment business, no less.

A few years ago, both Andrew Davis, now thirty-six, and Chris Davis, now thirty-four, left their jobs at other investment firms to work for Davis Selected Advisers, the mutual fund company over which their father, Shelby Davis, presides as chief executive officer and chief investment officer. Andrew is manager of Davis Convertible Securities and Davis Real Estate funds, while brother Chris manages Davis New York Venture and Selected American Shares funds. Is there a rivalry between the brothers? "No, I'm just better than he is," jokes Andrew from his office in New Mexico. "Seriously, Chris and I worked all that out before we joined the firm. I am one of the larger shareholders in Chris's fund, and I want him to do well."

Brother Chris, based in New York (a little distance never

hurts in any family), echoes that sentiment: "We're very close. We went through a period of being very competitive, but that resolved itself. We have an incredible advantage in this business based on the level of trust we have with each other."

What the brothers also share is a commitment to an investing philosophy—a buy-and-hold style of value investing—and the experience of being schooled in investing by two first-rate instructors. Their father founded New York Venture Fund in 1969. Their grandfather Shelby Cullom Davis was a legendary investor who borrowed $100,000 in 1947 to start a firm specializing in insurance stocks and turned it into a fortune worth some $800 million by the time he died in 1994. "My father never pushed us into the business, but he felt you had to learn to manage your money," says Chris Davis.

STREET SLANG<

LOAD
The sales charge on a mutual fund. A fund with a load is indeed weighed down when trying to reach for performance.

Early lessons included frequent discussions on the power of compound interest and dinner-table discussions about stocks. "My father and grandfather made investing accessible to us. They reduced it to a few simple things: stocks are companies, and companies are people and ideas," says Chris. "They also made us feel confident. You didn't need to be the smartest in your class to be a great investor, but you had to have the right disposition and the right attitude about investing."

As the boys got older they were encouraged to buy stock. "I think I was about ten when I bought my first stock. It was United Jersey Bank," says Andrew Davis. "I think it was a $9 stock at the time, and we sold it for $12. The biggest mistake I made was selling too early. The stock ended up in the 40s." He bought the stock after having a telephone discussion with the company's investor relations department. "I remember talking to my father about the company in simplistic terms. He and I put together a list of questions on a sheet of yellow paper, and I called the company. I can't imagine what that guy thought of this kid calling."

As teenagers and during their college years, both boys (along with their younger sister) spent summers working in their father's office, writing stock research reports for $100 each. They also sat in on meetings their father had with corporate managers. Chris's early investments included Transworld Music, a company that managed recorded music departments in stores, and VLI, a contraceptive manufacturer. "When I was sixteen, I would go through the annual reports in the library, and some things would catch my eye. As I remember, the contraceptive company was not a good investment."

Andrew's biggest disappointment as a young investor came with a stock he bought in his early twenties. "I invested in a Canadian gold-mining company. It turned out that they were fraudulently seeding their mines with gold flakes to make it appear there was more gold in there than met the eye," he says. "My grandfather used to say that management rarely lies to you, but they are often wrong. Well, this was an example where management lied. The stock held up for a while, but when the drop came, it didn't take long. The stock collapsed within about an hour. I found out about it reading the newspaper."

In hindsight, Andrew thinks he ignored some early warning signs. "I probably didn't understand the business as well as I could have. I don't know that I could have foreseen the fraud, but I did learn that if something sounds too good to be true, it probably is. This company had a story that they didn't even need the price of gold to rise in order to make money, that the amount of gold they were going to be able to pull out of the ground was going to grow precipitously." It gets back to a lesson drilled into the Davis boys early on. "Instead of imagining owning some stock, imagine owning the entire business," says Andrew. "If the return on that business is whatever income you have at the end of the day after keeping that business competitive, and if you conclude that buying the entire business would be worth it, then buying the stock will be, too. My grandfather always said there are a million ways to make money on Wall Street. There are value investors and momentum investors, and they can all work. The important thing is to know what you're good at. For me, the owning-the-entire-company argument is the one that makes the most sense."

The other lesson Andrew cites has come with maturity: understanding that it takes several things to make a stock a good buy. "When I was younger, I believed there was one answer to every problem, and you could say a company was a great company based on one fact. As you get older you realize it's really a mosaic; you have to have lots of pieces fitting together. You can't just have a company that makes great products, you have to have good management, and the stock has to be at the right price. You can buy stock in a great company, yet it might not be a great stock. If you pay a bad price for a great company, it's a very mediocre investment."

EACH OF THE INVESTORS PROFILED BECAME INTERESTED IN investing as kids or as young adults. Were they successful because they got an early start on investing? Or did they get Street wise early on because they had the sort of mind that understood and was enthralled by the market? No doubt it's a little of both. But what is clear is that investing is a skill you can improve with practice. And if experience is the best teacher, early experience amounts to a head start.

"There is still one other reason to invest through mutual funds rather than on your own. It gives you someone to blame if there's a screw-up."

RALPH WANGER IN
A ZEBRA IN LION COUNTRY

Mutual Respect: Funds

A STOCK IS TO A MUTUAL FUND AS:*

(a) a can of soda is to a six-pack.

(b) the Dallas Cowboys are to the NFL.

(c) a kitten is to a dog.

(d) a flower is to a garden.

*See box on page 134 for correct answer

IF YOU'VE EVER TAKEN THE SAT, YOU'LL IMMEDIATELY recognize the type of question above. The analogy question is a maddening staple of standardized tests. (If you haven't yet encountered quizzes like the one above, brace yourself. You will.) There's usually one answer that you can throw out immediately. (I hope I'm not giving anything away if I point out that (c) is not the way to go.) But then there are usually a couple of answers close enough to correct that you might be able to talk yourself into thinking they're right.

Analogies have a function. They can help you understand the relationship between different ideas. And as it happens, mutual funds can be best explained by pointing out what they do and don't have in common with stocks.

Mutual funds are a great invention. When you own shares in a mutual fund (and you buy shares—much like you would buy shares of stock), you and umpteen-thousand other investors jointly own a whole basketful of different stocks. The fund employs a professional money manager who buys and sells these stocks, and the value of your shares in the mutual fund goes up or down depending on whether the underlying stocks go up or down. Profits that are made in the fund are paid out to investors in the form of dividends, which shareholders can either take in cash or have automatically reinvested in the fund.

> STREET SMARTS<
>
> **Sage,** the excellent online mutual fund reference found on AOL (and soon to be on the Web), **posts a list of ten funds it thinks are ideal for kids** due to their low investment minimums. They are ASM Index 30, Babson Growth, Domini Social Equity, Fasciano Fund, MSB, Muhlenkamp, Nicholas, Pax World, Stein Roe Young Investor, and Strong Total Return. For more details about the funds, check out the Sage site, AOL keyword: Sage or at sageonline.com.

Mutual funds overcome some of the difficulties and disadvantages of owning individual stocks. Remember the whole problem of diversification from Chapter 2? Investing in several different stocks reduces your risk of losing money, because your money is spread out among different companies and industries. The idea is that while some stocks might slump, you can own enough different ones to make it unlikely they'll all be slumping at the same time. But the difficult thing about diversification, especially for the beginning investor, is that you may not have enough money to adequately diversify. As this was being written, General Electric was trading at about 124, IBM at 113, and McDonald's at 43. Just imagine if you had $1,000 to invest, and you were trying to buy twenty different stocks in those price ranges.

Buying a share in a mutual fund is a way to own a piece of dozens of stocks, rather than owning a small number of shares in just one or two stocks. See "The Mutual Fund Mix" on the following page for a glimpse of the stock holdings in Fidelity's Magellan Fund, one of the largest funds in the country.

A mutual fund can easily have fifty or a hundred stocks in its portfolio and can offer even a higher-risk investor some reassuring conservatism. "I have most of my money in individual stocks," says eighteen-year-old high school senior Jason Orlovsky. "But my parents wanted me to move some of the money I've made into more conservative mutual funds because I'm planning to use it for college."

Many mutual fund companies have programs that make things even easier for a small investor, with low minimums (the lowest amount you can open an account with—sometimes as little as $250 or $500, or even lower in kid-friendly funds) and automatic monthly investment programs. With an automatic program, you can arrange to have as little as $20 a month wired out of your checking account into a mutual fund. A regular investment program like that can't be beat.

You may have every intention of putting a little aside every month and investing, but if it's done automatically, it's more likely to actually get done. When you're studying for final exams in high school or college, the last thing you're going to want to think about is "Did I send in my monthly investment?" With a mutual fund, you can come closer to putting your investment discipline on autopilot.

You also get professional management. With a fund, you get a portfolio manager whose job it is to research the market and

The Mutual Fund Mix

THE BEST WAY TO DEMYSTIFY MUTUAL FUNDS is to peek into their portfolios and see what they're holding in their shopping baskets of stocks.

Fidelity's Magellan Fund is one of the biggest funds in the country, with a cool $100 *billion* in assets. The fund, which has a load, or sales charge, of 3 percent up front, has returned 25 percent a year over the past five years (slightly below the S&P 500 five-year average of 27.88 percent.) Magellan, named for the explorer, holds hundreds of securities, but below are the ten stocks that make up the largest percentage of the portfolio as of early 2000. The fund describes itself as a "growth" fund, which means it invests in stocks that it thinks will rise in price, as opposed to stocks that pay high dividends. A look at the largest holdings confirms this.

STOCK	PERCENTAGE OF MAGELLAN PORTFOLIO
General Electric	4.17%
Microsoft	4.11%
MCI Worldcom	2.38%
America Online	2.28%
Home Depot	2.22%
Cisco Systems	2.03%
Merck & Co.	2.01%
IBM	1.88%
Citigroup, Inc.	1.74%
Wal-Mart Stores	1.67%

SOURCE: BLOOMBERG L.P.

pick stocks, bonds, or whatever other financial assets are in the fund. Presumably that person can do a better job than you can of picking individual stocks, and can certainly devote more time to the job. It's never a good idea to completely ignore your personal finances, but we're all busy. We may not want to actively manage a portfolio of stocks, with the burden of keeping track of daily stock-price fluctuations and breaking news on different companies. At a mutual fund, someone else is handling that—for a fee, of course. Mutual funds can carry a couple of different kinds of fees. It costs the fund money to pay a manager and to handle your investments. The administrative fees are charged as a percentage of your investment. This is called the **expense ratio.** These fees can't be avoided, but you can be careful to minimize them. Other fees, such as sales commissions, also called **loads**, can be avoided. We'll be talking more a little later about how to deal with fees.

There are more than 7,000 mutual funds out there, and picking one can be just as tricky as picking a stock. The first thing you need to do is decide what type of mutual fund you want to invest in. Remember our discussion of asset allocation in Chapter 2? Higher potential earnings means higher risk. A mutual fund full of hot new Internet IPO stocks is obviously at a greater risk for a drop in value than a fund full of corporate blue chips, though the high-tech fund may zoom upward faster, too.

Different varieties of funds have different risk-and-return profiles. In order to choose a fund, you first need to know what categories of funds are available. The Investment Company Institute, which is a trade and lobbying association made up of mutual fund companies, classifies mutual funds into thirty-three investment objective categories. Below is a simplified—and abridged—list of the types of mutual funds available.

STOCK FUNDS INVEST IN—WOULD YOU BELIEVE—STOCKS. Below are some of the different types of stock funds.

>>**Growth funds** are invested in companies whose sales and profits (and so, presumably, their stock prices) are poised to grow. These stocks are not chosen for their dividends; they are chosen in the hope that their share prices will go up a lot. There are subcategories of growth funds, such as **aggressive growth funds.** Any time you see the word aggressive in connection with investing, think risk. These are stocks that are seen to have more potential for both risk and return, such as stocks right after their initial public offering, or companies going through difficulties.

>>**Growth and income funds** invest in companies they think will see both a stock price rise and some dividend payments, and in a mix of companies that will do one or the other.

>>**Income-equity funds** invest in companies they think will pay good dividends.

>>**International funds** and **global funds** sound like the same thing, don't they? But there's an important difference. International funds invest in stocks of companies outside of the United States; global funds include companies with U.S. operations.

>>**Precious metal funds** buy shares in companies that mine or produce metals, such as gold.

BOND FUNDS INVEST IN BONDS. WITHIN THIS GROUP, AS WITH stock funds, there are several types, named by the kinds of bonds they invest in—**corporate bond funds, U.S. government bond funds, municipal bond funds** (which invest in bonds free from federal or state tax), **global bond funds, Ginnie Mae funds** (a nickname for GNMA, or Government National Mortgage Association; these funds invest in mortgage securities that are guaranteed by the government), and **high-yield bond funds** (which invest in more risky bonds).

>>**Stock and bond funds, or balanced funds,** invest in a

mix of stocks and bonds, trying to obtain growth and income conservatively.

>>**Money market funds** invest in securities called by the obscure-sounding name "short-term debt instruments." These are things like U.S. government securities (big denominations of government bonds with a short maturity) and highly rated corporate debt (safe corporate bonds). These funds are almost a substitute for a checking account, and like bank accounts, they pay interest. (That interest rate is usually higher than you would get on a bank savings or checking account.) Shares are priced at $1 each; the interest rate fluctuates. Although your money isn't guaranteed by the government (as it would be in a bank), there has never yet been an instance when an investor has lost money in a money market fund.

>>**Index funds** have grown extremely popular in recent years. An index fund buys only the stocks of companies in a particular index, such as the S&P 500 or the Dow Jones Industrial Average. The idea is to "buy the market" and mimic the return of the whole market, instead of trying to buy winning stocks. Another appeal of index funds is they have low management fees, since you're not paying an active manager (nobody has to choose stocks for the portfolio, since it consists of the stocks in an index). Year after year, index funds have outperformed most managed funds. There is a fund for practically every conceivable index, including small-cap index funds, which invest in smaller companies (a group that can see greater growth).

>>**Tax-free funds** invest in certain government securities that provide tax-free income. The return is lower than that of corporate bonds, but for people who have a large income and pay high tax rates, it may make sense to take a lower, tax-free return. These can be designed to be free from both federal and state tax . . . with a few exceptions. Tax-free funds aren't necessarily tax free all the time. The dividends are tax free, but if an investor sells shares, he or she might have taxable capital gains.

The fund manager might also sell securities and trigger a capital gain, which is passed on to shareholders, and tax-free funds can also be taxable for some wealthy shareholders who are subject to something called "federal alternative minimum tax." Taxes are never simple.

>>**Sector funds** invest in stocks in only one particular industry, like technology or health care companies. Invariably when you see lists of the best performing and worst performing mutual funds, sector funds are at the top and the bottom of the lists. At any time, certain industries may be booming while others are in the dumps. Sector funds should never be used as a general all-purpose investment, since they offer the opposite of diversification, concentration. Usually investors buy sector funds when they want to make a bet on a single industry. See "Flavors of Sector Funds" on pages 122–123 for some of the industries that sector funds are available in.

>>**Open-end funds and closed-end funds** differ in the number of shares available to investors and how they are bought and sold. Most funds are open-end funds. Open-end funds will sell as many shares as buyers want. You typically buy shares of an open-end fund by calling the management company, getting and reading the required paperwork, and sending in your money. The classic open-end fund isn't traded on a stock exchange.

By contrast, closed-end funds have a fixed number of shares, and so the shares can trade above or below the net asset value of a fund, based on supply and demand. Closed-end funds trade on an exchange in the same way stocks do. Sometimes an open-end fund can, confusingly, be temporarily closed to new investors. That happens when an open-end fund manager or company thinks too much money is flowing into a fund for the manager to effectively invest it all. But the open-end fund doesn't then become a closed-end fund. There are only a few hundred closed-end funds in existence.

>>**Load and no load funds** differ in how they are sold. Load funds are sold through brokers, who, naturally, have to be paid for the work of selling them to consumers. The load is usually a percentage of the consumer's investment—typical loads are 2 percent, 3 percent, or 5 percent of the investment. These sales charges are deducted when you buy a fund, so if you invest $1,000 in a 3-percent-load fund, only $970 is actually being invested. There are also **back-end loads**, where there's no charge to buy a fund, but there is a charge to sell your shares. Typically that back-end load is on a sliding scale—the longer you own the fund, the lower it goes. After perhaps five years the sales charge may disappear altogether.

Studies have shown that load funds don't outperform no-load funds. Which should you buy? Let's make it easy: I see no reason ever to buy a load fund.

DISADVANTAGES OF MUTUAL FUNDS

MUTUAL FUNDS COST MONEY, BEYOND THE PER-SHARE PRICE of the fund. First, there's the load, or the up-front sales charge that investors less savvy than you might be induced to pay.

But even no-load funds charge annual fees, and some also charge 12b-1 fees, which pay for the fund's marketing expenses

A Term You Need to Know

NET ASSET VALUE (NAV) is like a daily stock price. It is the price of one share of a mutual fund. It rises and falls with the prices of all the stocks the fund owns. If you want to know what you can sell your mutual fund for today, you look in the paper (or online) and check the NAV.

Flavors of Sector Funds

SECTOR FUNDS ARE A RISKIER SUBSET of the mutual fund world. They are funds that invest only in one particular type of business. You might buy one if you knew you wanted to own some stocks in a certain industry—say, the oil and gas business—but had no idea which stocks to buy.

They are riskier because they are less diversified than other mutual funds—all their eggs are in one industry basket, and if that industry is having trouble, a sector fund will show it. If you choose to invest in a sector fund (remember, you can always buy stock in Exxon Mobil rather than an energy fund), it should constitute a small part of your portfolio. Many fund families sell sector funds; typically they might have an energy fund, a gold or precious metals fund, and a health care industry fund. Fidelity, one of the biggest fund companies in the country, has dozens of sector funds in its Select Portfolios fund group. Some of the industries represented by funds include biotechnology, construction and housing, gold, health care, regional banks, retailing, and industrial equipment.

to attract new shareholders. (These 12b-1 fees are especially controversial, since many investors feel that they should not be charged for the money their fund spends selling more shares to other investors.) All of these expenses drain money from your investment assets, so a smart investor looks for a fund with low expenses.

How low? I wish I could give you a hard-and-fast expense ratio number (which is a way to measure and compare the actual expenses of any given fund). But expenses vary according to category. Average annual fees range anywhere from a low

Socially Conscious Funds

THERE ARE MUTUAL FUNDS which have adopted an investment philosophy of not investing in certain types of companies that shareholders might object to. These are called
"socially conscious" mutual funds. A typical socially conscious fund might refrain from investing in tobacco or liquor
companies or firms that own casinos. That fund may appeal
to someone who objects to smoking, gambling, or drinking
alcohol. That way investors aren't supporting an activity
with their investment dollars that they are fundamentally
opposed to.

There are several socially conscious funds; before you
invest, check them out carefully to make sure you agree
with their philosophy, and also to make sure they have
good investment performance. It's possible to do well while
doing good.

of 0.2 percent to perhaps 1.5 percent of your investment. The
low end is for index funds, which have among the lowest
expenses, since they're not actively managed. The most expensive funds to manage are typically international or emerging-
market funds. In her book *The New Commonsense Guide to
Mutual Funds* (Bloomberg Press, $15.95), author Mary
Rowland recommends looking for managed funds with expenses of less than 0.75 percent. The chart on the following page is
from a mutual fund prospectus, and it shows you how fees are
illustrated for prospective investors.

Another disadvantage of mutual funds is the tax complications that can come with them. While your trusty fund manager is picking stocks and buying and selling them, the fund is
generating income—both from stock dividends and from capi-

The Cost of a Mutual Fund

YOU DON'T GET ALL THOSE mutual fund management services for free. Funds charge operating expenses, which are disclosed clearly and in language even a nonlawyer can understand, in the mutual fund's prospectus, which is sent out to prospective shareholders. Below is a fee table from USAA's First Start Growth Fund prospectus. The bottom two rows tell you the effect of the operating expenses on a $1,000 investment in the fund, a number that drives home the actual cost of the fees. Fund expenses come out of the fund's assets and are reflected in the share price and dividends—you don't pay separate fees. The "Other Expenses" here include custodian and transfer agent fees. They have been estimated for the Fund's first year of operation. All of the figures below are calculated as a percentage of average net assets.

Management Fees	0.75%
12b-1 Fees	None
Other Expenses (estimated)	0.67%
Total Fund Operating Expenses	1.42%

Effects of Fees on Your Investment

YOU WOULD PAY THE FOLLOWING expenses on a $1,000 investment in this fund, assuming a 5 percent annual return and redemption (cashing out your shares) at the end of the periods shown.

1 year	$14
3 years	$45

tal gains. The fund "distributes" income to its shareholders, the same way a dividend is declared with a common stock. As we mentioned earlier, you owe tax on the fund's distribution, even if you had your portion reinvested. When you do sell fund shares, you need to figure out what the shares cost you originally so you can report how much they went up. That might be tricky if you bought some of the shares piecemeal, month by month at varying prices, through a reinvestment plan. It's the same when you own individual stocks, but if you're managing individual stocks, you have more control over when to buy and sell and are able to time capital gains better.

However, the disadvantages of mutual funds that I've detailed aren't reasons not to buy mutual funds—they're just reasons to buy carefully.

HOW TO CHOOSE A FUND

1. Decide what your objectives are and how much risk you can tolerate. Do you need the money for college in a year or two and therefore want something fairly safe? Stay away from the aggressive growth funds and steer yourself to perhaps a conservative bond fund. Do you think you won't need the money for a long time? Then you can be more aggressive and take more risk.

2. Once you've decided what category of fund you want to be in, start looking for a specific fund in that group. Below are some guidelines for looking for a good fund.

3. Check *Morningstar Mutual Funds* or *Value Line* (available in libraries and online at **www.morningstar.com**) to see what funds are highly ranked in comparison with others with the same investment objectives. (You wouldn't compare a bond fund with a growth and income stock fund.) Look to see how they have been ranked over a period of at least three years; five or ten years is even better. Also, you should look at a benchmark

Benchmark Your Fund

A MUTUAL FUND PROSPECTUS, the booklet filled with legalese you receive before you buy mutual fund shares, is worth reading. In the prospectus is information about the fund's performance and a benchmark to gauge that performance by. Below is fund performance information for Stein Roe's Young Investor Fund. The S&P 500 index number and the Lipper Peer Group Average allow you to judge this fund against its peers.

Average Annual Total Returns

	1 YR	3 YRS	5 YRS	LIFE OF FUND
Stein Roe Young Investor Fund*	24.12%	16.63%	24.76%	23.17%
S&P 500 Index	27.79	25.09	25.03	23.77
Lipper Peer Group Average	41.88	19.93	20.86	19.38

*STEIN ROE[SM] YOUNG INVESTOR[SM] FUND (SRYIX) FUND PERFORMANCE (AS OF SEPTEMBER 30, 1999)

for the fund. "If it's a small-cap fund, look to a small-cap index," says Stewart Welch, a Birmingham, Alabama, financial planner. "The idea is that they should outdo the benchmark—otherwise you might as well buy the benchmark." A fund prospectus will give you an example of how it has performed in comparison with a benchmark, as you can see by the chart above.

4. Narrow down your choices to the top few funds. Morningstar has its famous "star system" of ranking mutual funds: as with movie and restaurant reviews, the more stars the better. "When I decided to look for a mutual fund, I was looking for a growth and income fund that was ranked four or five stars by Morningstar," says sixteen-year-old Matt Wickert, of Newark, Delaware.

5. Disqualify any funds that aren't no-load with low expenses.

6. Call the fund companies to get a prospectus for each fund you're looking at. A prospectus is the thick, sleep-inducing document that you must look over before you invest. It tells you all sorts of things about the fund. Now required is an especially helpful table that details all fees charged by a fund and how they affect returns. You can see an example of such a table on page 124.

7. See how long the fund manager has been there. If the manager is new, it's not fair to give him or her credit for a fund's superior ten-year performance. The prospectus should tell you how long the current manager has been there.

8. Understand that—as mutual fund prospectuses will always say—past performance is no guarantee of future returns. Money invested in mutual funds isn't guaranteed or insured, even if you have bought a fund through a bank. (Not long ago a survey of adult investors showed that a high percentage had the misimpression that because they bought their mutual fund in a bank, it was insured in the same way that bank deposits of up to $100,000 are insured by the federal government.)

9. Once you've bought, keep an eye on the fund to see if its performance stays solid. "We normally give funds about a three-year rope," says financial planner Stewart Welch. "You expect to have some underperformance, and we take a long view, but we don't want to see the manager consistently underperforming the benchmark."

KID-FRIENDLY MUTUAL FUNDS

YOUR GENERATION IS A MEGAMARKET THAT COMPANIES—including financial services firms—are eager to sell to. Not only do you have money to spend now, while you're not yet into your

A Chat with a Kid-Friendly Fund Manager

CURT ROHRMAN IS THE PORTFOLIO MANAGER of USAA First Start Growth Fund, a kid-friendly mutual fund that was started on August 1, 1997. It's his job to choose which stocks the fund buys. In the case of First Start, the stocks have to qualify on two counts:

1. They have to be companies that provide products or services that kids are familiar with. Like several of the other kid-friendly funds, First Start has decided to focus on this group of companies.

2. As with any fund manager, Rohrman has to buy stocks that will produce a good return for the fund (or ultimately he's going to be looking for another job!). As of this writing, the fund's stocks include McDonald's, the Gap, PepsiCo, Microsoft, Walt Disney, and Clear Channel Communications, which owns about 200 radio stations across the country. Although these companies certainly don't cater exclusively to kids, Rohrman felt they were recognizable to them. "Kids today are outstanding consumers," he says. "Some adults still think of kids and money in terms of kids spending nickels to buy candy. But these days there's so much information thrown at them, whether through the Internet or on TV. They know what's going on, and the stock market is part of it all."

Rohrman has a column called "Ask Curt" in the fund's monthly newsletter to shareholders, *First Start News*. In it he responds to questions sent by kids via postage-paid postcards. "I get a

twenties, but corporations are trying to make lifelong customers out of you. Marketing research tells them that kids—all consumers, in fact—form loyalties to certain brands early on and then stick with them for years.

hundred or so cards every week," says Rohrman. "I run other funds, and if I get a specific question from a shareholder once over a period of three months, it's unusual."

Many of the questions ask why the fund doesn't own a particular stock. Sometimes his answer is "We do," as in the case of Mattel; sometimes it's "I don't think it's a good investment right now because it's priced too high," as in the case of Coca-Cola; and sometimes it's "We can't," as in the case of Ty, the company that makes Beanie Babies, because it's privately held and doesn't sell stock. Once in a while, a question will surprise even Rohrman. "We don't own stocks in tobacco, alcohol, and gaming [gambling] companies because we don't think these should be in a fund for kids, but I got a question from a kid once who said that he really liked Coors Beer, asking if there was another fund at USAA that owns stock in it!" he says.

Two of the stock suggestions Rohrman received from shareholders motivated him to buy the stocks for the fund. "I got a question from a kid asking why I didn't own AMC Entertainment, which has movie theaters," he says. "I started answering him as to why I didn't own it, and as I did that, I thought, 'I really ought to buy it.' " Another kid-motivated buy was Pixar, the company that made the movies *A Bug's Life* and *Toy Story*. "It had been on my radar screen for a while, but it was a question from a kid that made me take another look and buy it," Rohrman says.

So it's not surprising that several companies sell mutual funds specifically targeted to kids. It's a great way to provide a ready-made product for parents or grandparents who want you to learn about investing and also want to put away a little

How to Check Mutual Fund Quotations

AS WITH STOCKS, one of the great things about mutual funds is that you can check the value of your investment in the newspaper regularly and easily. (If you had all your money invested in Beanie Babies, you wouldn't have that luxury.) Below is a guide on how to read a mutual fund listing to see how your fund is doing.

| | | | Net | YTD | |
D et	Name	NAV	Chg	%ret	Nan
).2	DSI Dv	8.60	– 0.14	– 1.6	Em
).7	DSI LM	8.75	– 0.02	– 0.2	En
).9	FMASmCo	13.68	– 0.36	– 2.6	Ec
.6	FPACres	12.73	– 0.22	– 1.7	FL
.4	HansonEq	12.83	– 0.19	– 1.5	Ec
?.4	HEITREAd p	7.94	– 0.10	– 1.2	H
).2	USChina	6.17	+ 0.19	+ 3.2	H
.8	WldGld	8.14	– 0.05	– 0.6	Ir
.5	USGlbLdrs	25.33	– 0.67	– 2.6	L
2.5	**USAA Group:**				P
2.5	AgvGt	55.04	– 0.11	– 0.2	R
2.5	BalStra	15.53	– 0.11	– 0.7	T
.5	CA Bd	10.15	– 0.04	– 0.4	T
N	CrnstStr	25.78	– 0.20	–0.8	
N	EmgMkt	10.93	+ 0.08	+ 0.7	
	FStrtGr	16.91	+ 0.09	+ 0.2	V
?	GNMA	9.35	– 0.05	– 0.5	
	Gold	5.94	– 0.04	– 0.7	N

Name

NAV (16.91)

Net Chg (+0.09)

YTD %ret (+0.2)

Name: Mutual funds are listed alphabetically first by the name of the fund family (such as USAA Group) and then by abbreviations of the individual fund names (FStrtGr, for example, is First Start Growth).

NAV: Net asset value, which is the current share price.

Net Chg: Net change, which is the change in price—up or down—since yesterday.

YTD %ret: Year-to-date percentage return, which is how much the fund is up or down since the beginning of the year.

money for you. If the mutual fund company is lucky, you'll be so happy with your experience that you'll continue to use its services when you're an adult. Financial services firms suspect—with justification—that kids who are interested in investing when they're young will be affluent consumers in years to come. All that sounds more than a little cynical, but it's realistic. Companies will tell you they're simply interested in educating young investors, but at the end of the day, it's important to remember that any company is looking to move some product.

Don't get me wrong. That doesn't mean these funds aren't a good idea—I think they're a great concept. But you need to understand how they came to be.

"We started our fund in April 1984," says Marilyn Morrison, spokesperson for Stein Roe Mutual Funds' Young Investor Fund. "About 75 percent of account holders are under the age of eighteen. We have parents and grandparents setting up accounts, but there are also young shareholders who invest money they've earned baby-sitting or by doing chores."

The kid-friendly funds all have a few things in common. Most have a philosophy of investing in companies that make products or provide services for kids—things like Pepsi or toy-maker Mattel. Of course, that can be a pretty broad category and can encompass firms like Microsoft or America Online, both of which are no doubt used by kids but are hardly thought of as "kiddie stocks."

Usually these funds also have lower minimum investments than other funds in the firm's stable, and they have automatic investment plans that allow small—like $20 or $25 a month—transfers from your checking or savings account into the mutual fund.

Several funds have educational materials they send to shareholders. Some of the material would probably be better suited to your younger brothers or sisters than to a teen, such as the coloring books that some fund firms send out. However, a lot of the educational material is entertaining and informative no matter what your age.

Stein Roe Mutual Funds, the firm that pioneered the kids' fund idea, sends out a quarterly newsletter, *Dollar Digest,* to shareholders of Young Investor Fund. *Dollar Digest* includes interviews with chief executive officers of companies that Young Investor owns shares in. Microsoft's Bill Gates and Jill Barad, former head of Mattel, both have been featured in *Dollar Digest.* "We have some shareholders who are adults who have purchased the fund to get the educational materials so they themselves can bone up on investing," says Morrison. A similar publication is USAA's newsletter for underage shareholders, *First Start News.* Among its features is a question and answer column by the fund manager. These newsletters are available to shareholders only, but if you want to see a copy, call the funds (listed below) and ask for a prospectus and an issue of the newsletter. Funds are happy to help possible customers.

Below are some details on the different funds.

>>**American Express IDS New Dimensions** (ticker INNDX)
(800-437-4332; www.americanexpress.com).
Minimum investment: $500, or $50 a month.
Investment objective: Large-cap growth.
Load: 5 percent.

This fund has the advantage of having a longer performance record than some of the other kid funds; American Express IDS started the New Dimensions fund back in 1967. The fund is now part of the company's "Kids, Parents, and Money" program, which was instituted in 1997. "This was already a strong growth fund, and it had several stocks that kids could relate to," says Leila Erlandson of American Express Financial Advisors. The fund manager doesn't pick stocks with an eye to companies kids might be familiar with, but there are those types of holdings in the portfolio. Other educational material provided to families includes *A Busy Parent's Guide to Teaching Kids About Money* and a booklet for elementary-age kids called *Kate and Kenny's Marvelous Money Adventure*. The fund's minimum is lower if you invest through the kids' program. Note the 5 percent load.

>>INVESCO
(800-525-8085; www.invesco.com).
Minimum investment: $250, or $25 a month.
Investment objective: Program includes four funds
with different objectives, described below.
Load: None.

INVESCO's "Driving into Your Financial Future" program makes four funds more kid-friendly by lowering the minimum investment required to $250, or $25 a month. The four funds and their objectives are the following: Blue Chip Growth (ticker symbol FLRFX), a moderately aggressive stock fund; Invesco Endeavor (ticker symbol IVENX), which the firm describes as a "very aggressive" stock fund; Equity Income Fund (ticker symbol FIIIX), whose portfolio is 75 percent stocks and 25 percent bonds; and Select Income (ticker symbol FBDSX), which is a corporate bond fund. Invesco conducts seminars on investing for kids in its hometown of Denver but doesn't currently send educational material to its young shareholders.

>>Monetta Express
(800-666-3882; www.monetta.com).
Minimum investment: $250, or $25 per quarter.
Investment objective: Program includes seven funds
with different objectives.
Load: None, but there are 12b-1 fees.

Participants get a prize for beginning the Monetta Express program for kids—a bean-filled plush toy train engine named

Answer Box (from page 113)

NOW THAT YOU'VE LEARNED THE BASICS of mutual funds, what is the correct answer to the question at the beginning of the chapter? A stock is to a mutual fund as:

(a) a can of soda is to a six-pack.
(b) the Dallas Cowboys are to the NFL.
(c) a kitten is to a dog.
(d) a flower is to a garden.

For anyone who is still in doubt, the answer is (d). But you knew that, didn't you? For those interested, let's weed out the other possibilities. (c) is the ridiculous, let's-see-if-this-one-has-a-pulse answer. The correct answer isn't (a) because all the sodas in a six-pack—the parts of the larger whole—are the same, which isn't true in a stock mutual fund. And the answer isn't (b) because although the NFL is made up of several football teams, they couldn't exist without the league, and as you now know, you can invest in stocks without ever going near a mutual fund. That leaves (d). And a garden is like a mutual fund because it has many different types of flowers. In fact, variety is what gives a garden its appeal—different flowers bloom at different times, just as certain stocks may do well at some times and not at others.

Steady Eddy—and as kids make additional investments in their fund, they collect plush train cars. When they've reached $5,000, they will have collected all seven cars. "We're trying to impress on kids today that it takes time to build wealth," says Robert Bacarella, president of the fund. "I've had people come up and ask if they could give us $5,000 to collect all the cars at once, but we've said no. We want them to do it in increments." Also geared toward kids are the different educational materials that come with the program, including stories that tackle various economic concepts and an activity book and crayons.

>>**Stein Roe Young Investor** (ticker SRYIX) and **Stein Roe Growth Investor** (ticker SRGIX)
(800-338-2550; **www.younginvestor.com**).
Minimum investment: $1,000 for a custodial account, or $100 minimum with $50 per month thereafter.
Investment objective: Large-cap growth.
Load: None.

These are the best known and largest of the kiddie funds. Young Investor and the newer Growth Investor have the same portfolio; the difference is that Growth Investor comes without the educational material that accompanies Young Investor. For kids in the Young Investor program, materials include the *Dollar Digest* newsletter, an activity book, and additional information about investing. There is also a yearly essay contest for shareholders, who are asked to write on topics such as "Who is my role model."

>>**USAA First Start Growth** (ticker UFSGX)
(800-235-8377).
Minimum investment: $250, or $20 a month.
Investment objective: Large cap growth.
Load: None.

Like Stein Roe, USAA's First Start invests in stocks kids are familiar with. Investors receive *First Start News,* a quarterly newsletter. Unlike some USAA products, which require a family member to be in the military, there are no such requirements to buy into this fund.

"There were more sellers than buyers."

J. P. MORGAN SR.,
WHEN ASKED WHY THE STOCK
MARKET HAD FALLEN
THE PREVIOUS DAY

Bear Wrestling

IF YOU WERE BORN AFTER 1982, YOU'VE NEVER SEEN A SUS-
tained bear market—an extended period when stock prices are
generally falling. But someday you will.

The Dow Jones Industrial Average ended 1999 at 11,497, up
25.2 percent for the year. It was the fifth consecutive year that
the Dow increased by more than 10 percent. That uninterrupt-
ed upswing started way back on October 11, 1990. At that point
the Dow began its climb from 2,365 all the way up to and
through the 10,000 barrier, which it pierced on March 29,
1999. That's heady stuff, and it can distort the expectations even
of older investors. "With the recent history of the market, even
adults who have lived through a bear market have come to
expect 15 percent earnings a year. They don't have a memory of
a bear market," says Kathleen Stepp, a financial planner with
Stepp & Rothwell, in Overland Park, Kansas, who has made

several appearances in *Worth Magazine*'s yearly listing of the best financial planners in the country.

But 15 percent or 20 percent yearly returns are far enough above the historical averages that it's unreasonable to expect them to continue. In the future it is likely that returns will be smaller. Although we have no reason to think a market downturn is imminent, if you are a long-term investor—in this for forty or fifty years—the time will undoubtedly come when you see a real bear market.

Exactly what is a bear market? Different analysts have different definitions, but it's generally agreed that when the market (as measured by the Dow Jones Industrial Average) drops 20 percent, 25 percent, or more from its high, a bear market is upon us. Another term you may hear is stock market "correction": a more gentle slide, in which prices decline by 10 percent.

It's been a long time since what could honestly be called a bear market—since 1990, when the Dow Jones Industrial Average dropped 21 percent (just barely qualifying as a bear!). And that decline was short-lived, passing in a few months.

As this is being written in May 2000, the market is currently in a nasty downturn. The Dow is down 9.3 percent for the year, while the Nasdaq index, which saw an unprecedented rise in 1999, is down 22.2 percent.

Perhaps the market will continue to decline and someday we will all be talking about the bear market of 2000. Certainly many observers have been predicting a downturn, as stock prices have risen higher than most people thought possible over the last few years. Or maybe this is a temporary downturn, and investors will wish they had loaded up on stocks before the market shot up again. There are currently plenty of "market experts" appearing on the television financial news shows who predict either of these two possibilities. As painful as it has been for investors, this downturn doesn't yet qualify as a bear market— and certainly not as a prolonged bear.

Many investors therefore may not fully appreciate what history shows us: that contrary to the experiences of the last decade or so, stock prices can assuredly go down—and stay down—for a good long while.

Take the period from early January 1973 to early December 1974—a period of nearly two years. The Dow dropped 45 percent before turning up again. And of course the bear to beat all bears was the Great Depression. In the 1929 stock market crash, the Dow tumbled two consecutive days, October 28 and 29 (dropping 12.82 percent and 11.73 percent, respectively), and kicked off the Great Depression, which lasted until the 1940s, when defense spending for World War II got the economy going again. It took more than twenty years before the Dow again hit the heights it had hit in the late 1920s, before the crash.

The one crash you may have lived through, although you

> STREET SLANG

BEAR MARKET

A market with **falling stock prices.** Visualize a bear slapping its paw down to keep straight on the direction of a bear market. In a bear market, expect to see lots of newspaper and magazine headlines using bear puns, such as "hibernate" and "growl."

probably don't remember it, came in 1987. On "Black Monday," October 19, 1987, the Dow dropped 508 points, or 22.61 percent, in one day. (The story goes that Federal Reserve chair Alan Greenspan was flying cross-country that day, and when he landed he asked an aide how the market had closed. When told that the market had fallen 508, for an instant he relaxed, thinking it had dropped 508 basis points, or 5.08 points. A moment later he realized with horror that the decimal point belonged two places to the right.) For a comparable thing to happen with the Dow at current levels—say 10,500—it would have to drop, in one heart-stopping day, to 8,400.

Not all bear markets announce themselves with a crash.

Indeed, a crash sometimes marks the end of a bear period. A sustained market downturn often consists of a steady, sickening drift downward. Look again at the dismal market of 1973 and 1974. Although the market dropped 45 percent during that time, no one day ranks among the ten worst days in market history.

Some stock market commentators even speak of a "stealth bear," when the Dow stays up because the thirty stocks that make up the Dow Jones Industrial Average are up, but the broader universe of stocks is dropping.

Whatever their causes and duration, bear markets all have the same effect on investors, testing their patience and eroding their confidence along with their portfolio values. Most investors will tell you they're in the market for the long term. But the real test comes not when the market is regularly hitting new highs but when they see the value of their stocks drop and drop some more . . . and then drop even farther. That's when staying in the market, or even buying more shares, takes courage and faith and conviction.

"I remember in 1973 and 1974 my father sitting at the table talking about stocks and saying that he thought he bought them cheap, but they just keep getting cheaper," says Andrew Davis. His father, Shelby Davis, told his sons that a real bear market was when you wished you'd gone into the real estate business instead of investing.

The big question is: what should you do if you hit a bear market?

Remember to think long term. "One of the first things I do when I speak with new clients is to talk with them about the long-term rates of return," says Stewart Welch, an Alabama financial planner. "We tell them that historically the market has returned 11 percent a year over time. But we also tell clients, 'If you had given us $50,000 to invest in January 1973, by the end of two years your portfolio would have been worth only

$25,000. If you didn't panic and sell, over the next two years it came back to $50,000, but by then your money had been with us for four years, and you hadn't made any money.'" Since then, of course, that stake left invested in the market would have multiplied several times over. "Clients ask what will I do if the market is moving through a correction or a bear market," Welch says. "The right answer is 'Nothing.' The wrong answer is 'Panic.'"

Statistics back up Welch. If you had invested $1 in the S&P 500 at the end of 1925, you would have had $2,350.89 by the end of 1998, according to Ibbotson Associates. That's a compound annual growth rate of 11.2 percent, which is a healthy return over a period of seventy years. (The figures don't include taxes and do assume that you reinvest all dividends.)

Teenagers and young investors should take comfort from the fact that—as we've said—time is on your side. If your stock holdings drop in a bear market, you have time to recoup your losses in the earnings years ahead of you.

Staying put and doing nothing aren't the only useful strategies to know about if you're concerned about an eventual bear market. Here are specific recommendations to make sure you're not badly mauled.

>>Bear market survivors usually have invested wisely to begin with. Diversify your holdings. "I tell adults, 'I know you want to have 100 percent of your money in AOL, but we want you to have some in bonds, too. They're boring, but they're safer,'" says Kathleen Stepp. "For kids, we like to be 100 percent in stocks, but we would be diverse about the kinds of stocks. We'd have large cap, small cap, and international stocks. It's even possible we might have some bonds, if we owned a balanced mutual fund."

>>Buy stocks that you wouldn't mind holding for a long time. This, too, is basic advice but is worth repeating. Solid companies with reasonable stock prices tend to rebound nicely after a bear market.

What's in the Dow?

THE DOW JONES INDUSTRIAL AVERAGE (DJIA) was concocted to give the public a sense of whether the stock market was generally going up or down. Although only twelve stocks were included in the average when it began in 1896, by 1928 the index had grown to include thirty stocks. Today it still includes thirty stocks, but the editors of *The Wall Street Journal* periodically add or drop companies from the list in order to make the DJIA more representative of the economy. Below is a list of the stocks currently in the Dow.

COMPANY	TICKER SYMBOL
Alcoa	AA
American Express Co.	AXP
AT&T	T
Boeing Co.	BA
Caterpillar Inc.	CAT
Citigroup Inc.	C
Coca-Cola Co.	KO
DuPont Co.	DD
Eastman Kodak Co.	EK
Exxon Mobil Corp.	XOM

>>**Don't keep any money in the stock market that you need in the next few years.** A market downturn can turn traumatic if the money with which you were going to pay college tuition next year evaporates in the downturn. You will need to panic and sell to make sure you don't lose even more. Says Welch, "We tell clients, 'Whatever money you are going to need in less than five years shouldn't be in the market, but any money you don't need for five years absolutely should be in the market.'"

COMPANY	TICKER SYMBOL
General Electric Co.	GE
General Motors Corp.	GM
Home Depot Inc.	HD
Honeywell International Inc.	HON
Hewlett-Packard Co.	HWP
International Business Machines Corp.	IBM
Intel Corp.	INTC
International Paper Co.	IP
J.P. Morgan & Co.	JPM
Johnson & Johnson	JNJ
McDonald's Corp.	MCD
Merck & Co.	MRK
Microsoft Corp.	MSFT
Minnesota Mining & Manufacturing Co.	MMM
Philip Morris Cos.	MO
Procter & Gamble Co.	PG
SBC Communications Inc.	SBC
United Technologies Corp.	UTX
Wal-Mart Stores Inc.	WMT
Walt Disney Co.	DIS

>>Keep some money in cash equivalents, which are safe and liquid, meaning you can quickly and reliably get to your money if you want it. If you think a bear market is coming, putting some of your money into a money market account is a way of protecting its value and keeping cash available to buy stocks once their prices have dropped.

>>Stay humble during the bull market. "Don't confuse brains with a bull market" is an old Wall Street adage. Its mean-

ing is obvious: when the market is headed up, most stocks are headed up, so even if you didn't do a good job choosing stocks, the market will bail you out. The danger of a bull market is that you get overconfident and think you're a genius stock picker. That might encourage you to risk more than you otherwise would.

>>**Make sure you're not trading on margin.** In a falling market, margin traders can bet they'll be receiving **margin calls**—the notifications from a broker that the value of your **securities portfolio** (which is the collateral for your loan to buy more stock) has dropped. If you get a margin call you have two choices: put up more cash or watch your portfolio be sold out from under you. Even if you have faith the market is coming back and the patience to wait it out, if you're trading on margin and can't or don't want to shovel more money into your stock market account, your stocks will be sold. A margin account won't allow you to sit and wait for better days.

>>**If you want to limit losses on specific stocks, place stop-loss orders with your broker.** That means you specify a price at which your stocks are automatically sold—perhaps 20 percent below the level at which you bought them. That, of course, means that you might get sold out of a stock that will come back later, but it does limit your immediate losses.

LIVING THROUGH A SUSTAINED BEAR MARKET IS PROBABLY A little like having your heart broken. You can read about it all you want, but until it happens to you, it's tough to know what it really feels like and how you're going to react. It helps to keep a historical perspective—to know that you're not the first investor ever to live through a bad market, that this, too, will pass, and that the long-term direction of stocks is up.

"Talent wins games, but teamwork wins championships."

MICHAEL JORDAN

Joining the Club

ON THE FIRST SATURDAY OF EACH MONTH A GROUP OF
about fifteen kids, approximate ages eleven to eighteen, gather
in the basement of St. George's Episcopal Church in northwestern Washington, D.C. There they debate the merits of investing
in stocks like America Online, Lucent Technologies, Kmart,
Staples, Warner Lambert, and Allstate Corp. The kids belong to
St. George's Junior Investment Club (SGJIC), begun in 1996 by
Grafton Daniels, an eighty-eight-year-old retired stockbroker,
who has launched more than a dozen investment clubs over the
years. This one was originally started to help his twin sixteen-
year-old granddaughters learn about investing but has now
taken root and captured the interest of a whole group of young
investors in the community. The club, which started with each
kid making a $50 initial contribution and monthly $5 contributions thereafter, now manages a portfolio worth more than

$20,000. The average kid's share in that portfolio has grown (with the monthly contributions and investment returns) from the $50 initial stake to $776.58.

One recent Saturday morning the group was going through a familiar exercise: deciding how to invest the money in their treasury. The possibilities included adding to a Fannie Mae dividend reinvestment plan they participate in; buying stock in Carnival cruise lines (stock symbol CCL); and buying stock in Cisco Systems (CSCO), the maker of computer hardware and software for the Internet. As Daniels and a club member led the group through their analysis of Carnival and Cisco, the teens sat around tables, looking over Standard & Poor's stock reports and National Association of Investors Corp. (NAIC) stock analysis work sheets. Several of the kids were tapping numbers into their calculators as they looked over their work sheets. The teens debated the impact of some recent bad news for Carnival ("People aren't going to stop taking cruises," said their adviser) and the advisability of putting money into the dividend reinvestment plan (DRIP). "I think we should skip a month on the DRIP," said Joel Miles, age eighteen. Daniels pushed for the DRIP, suggesting that the whole point of such a plan was to invest small amounts on a regular basis. "Yeah, but if we think we could earn a better return someplace else, shouldn't we do that?" asked Miles. "We can go back to the DRIP next month.") When the vote came, the group's decision was to put some

> STREET SLANG<
> ## STREET NAME
> Sounds a bit like a police officer's term, but has an entirely innocent meaning. When you buy a stock and **don't take delivery of the stock certificate,** allowing your brokerage firm to hold it on your behalf, the stock is in "street name." Keeping stock in street name makes it easier to trade on short notice; you don't have to physically deliver the certificate to the broker's office if you want to sell.

money into the DRIP and also to buy stock in Carnival rather than Cisco, a choice based largely on Cisco's high stock price. The young investors questioned whether Cisco's stock would continue to rise so much in the future.

This group of investment-savvy teens is one of a burgeoning number of kid-friendly investment clubs in the country. Although no one keeps count of how many clubs involve teenagers, Jeffery Fox, director of youth programs for NAIC, thinks interest is growing. "There are family investing clubs, a handful of school investing clubs, and others, but because we don't keep track of the age of our members, we don't know how many teens are involved in clubs," he says. "We just started offering a youth membership about a year ago, and about 3,600 kids have signed up so far."

You may have heard of investment clubs from the publicity generated by the Beardstown Ladies, a group of older women who gained national fame with their best-selling books about the methods and superior performance of their investment club. The group later came under criticism when it turned out that the investment returns they had claimed included additional cash contributions from the group and therefore were not accurate. Still, their image—of being simultaneously folksy and Street wise—has stayed with them, their popularity has endured, and they continue to generate fascination with the idea of investment clubs. And—as is shown by the St. George's group above—investment clubs aren't just for adults. You can reap the same advantages that adults do.

In a typical adult investment club, each member chips in a set amount of money each month, and the group meets regularly to make decisions about how to invest their pooled funds. Members research stocks they think might be good investments and make presentations to the group about their stock ideas. The club then votes on whether or not to buy each stock and add it to their shared portfolio.

It's easy to imagine how much you can learn by participating

Dollar Cost Averaging

DOLLAR COST AVERAGING is a fancy name for a simple concept. It involves investing a regular, fixed amount of money, such as $25 a month. It's important not to try to "time" the market, trying to invest at precisely the moment when you think stock prices are about to take off, or to pull your money out of the market when you think there will be a downturn. Remember the "slow but steady" slogan. Dollar cost averaging has another big advantage: because you're spending a fixed amount of money each month rather than, say, buying a fixed number of shares each month, your cash will automatically buy more shares when stock prices are lower than when they're higher. This lowers your overall cost of investing.

in a group activity like this. While theoretically club members could study the subject by themselves, there's something about coming together as a group that both encourages and requires you to look more carefully at stocks. "It's a nice way to learn about investing," say Beth Hamm, who has run both youth and adult clubs in Grand Rapids, Michigan. "You have an exchange of information with other people who are enthusiastic about the subject."

Investment clubs also allow you to run a larger portfolio than you could on your own. Pooling your money with others, you can buy more stock than you would be able to otherwise and diversify more. The regular meetings—in which you contribute your monthly dues—also encourage you to continue investing at a steady clip through stock market ups and downs. That concept is known as **dollar cost averaging**.

And as with any club, there's a social element to investment clubs. "We try to do fun things to keep everyone's interest going," says Kaye Corrigan, a teacher in Naperville, Illinois, who runs a high school investment club. "Once a year we have a meeting at someone's house. We've gotten together for dinner with an investment club across town, and we have a holiday gift exchange that is a sort of swapping game."

Investment clubs that involve teens can take many forms. Many youth clubs don't invest with real money. As we've discussed, because kids legally aren't old enough to invest on their own, a youth investment club that deals with real money requires that accounts be set up in parents' names, with the stipulation that the kids get to make the investment decisions. Some schools shy away from sponsoring an activity that requires regular monetary contributions, fearing that the whole concept would be seen as exclusionary and elitist. Some teachers, too, are concerned that if students lost money in a school investment club, parents could complain that the teens were given bad investment advice.

But even teen investment clubs that don't use real cash find that organizing into a group can still be profitable and fun. The Bulls and Bears Club, for example, is a stock market club at Palos Verdes Peninsula High School in California. The group, which meets once or twice a month, includes about fifteen high school students, grades nine through twelve. Although the group is prohibited by school rules from investing real money, the students participate as a group in online investment contests. "Most of the students invest on their own, so when we meet as a club we talk about their investments and the market in general," says the group's current president, senior Heather Innes. "We always have CNBC on during our meetings, and we do research on the Internet and take a vote on what stocks we want to invest in." Among the club's best recent investment-contest stock picks was Yahoo; among its worst was Western Digital.

The investing club at Baraboo High School in Baraboo, Wisconsin, has a similar agenda. Thirty to forty kids, grades nine through twelve, meet once a week at 7:30 A.M. The kids, who organize themselves into groups of three to eight students, participate in a variety of online investment contests. "I ask each team member to come up with two stocks, and they research them and decide whether to put them into their portfolio," says adviser and math teacher Chris Labeots. "The kids all have a unit on economics in eighth grade and then a full semester on economics in ninth grade, so they have a working knowledge of the stock market. They come in knowing quite a bit about what makes the market move. I find that different teams will try different strategies. Some may buy all technology stocks, some all Internet stocks, or others may buy off the hot list that Yahoo has. Then they compare their performance with each other."

STREET SLANG<
TENDER OFFER
Nothing romantic implied here. It's a public invitation for stockholders to sell their shares, and is typically used in the takeover of a company. To "tender" the shares means to give them up or sell them.

One younger club that has attracted national attention is the Wall Street Whiz Kids, of St. Agnes Grammar School in Arlington, Massachusetts. The group, which was founded in 1990, is open to the school's eighth graders. Over the years the Wall Street Whiz Kids and their adviser, seventh grade teacher Joan Morrissey, have been written up in publications such as *The Wall Street Journal* and *USA Today* and have appeared on NBC's *Dateline* and been interviewed by Maury Povich. The kids appeared with Fidelity Investments' famed former money manager Peter Lynch in a video produced for the Securities and Exchange Commission on kids and investing. The Wall Street Whiz Kids also competed against Lynch in a stock-picking contest and beat him by a razor-thin 0.1 percent. The Wall Street Kids compete in various investment contests, as well as running their own paper portfolios.

The NAIC, mentioned at the beginning of this chapter, is a nonprofit investor education group that has helped thousands of investment clubs get their start. The group promotes a model club for students called the traveling investment club. In a traveling club, the group meets to choose stocks, and then each individual invests on his or her own. The stocks "travel" with the students. "In a traveling club a group of individuals get together every week or two to learn the basic concepts of investing and to run a paper portfolio," says Jeffery Fox of NAIC. "They select and analyze companies and mutual funds, and if individuals want to invest they can, and the securities are in their name, not in the club's name."

According to Fox, a traveling club neatly solves some common difficulties of student investment clubs. Because a club that invests real money has certain bookkeeping and tax accounting chores, sometimes it's difficult to find a teacher who will take on the job of being an adviser. "A traveling club is like any other investment club without the hassle of the red tape," says Fox. Another common difficulty of student investment clubs is the transient nature of students. "They're not around for many years," says Fox. "There are adult NAIC clubs where people have been members for thirty years, but students are only in high school for four. A traveling club doesn't have to worry about selling stocks or liquidating a portfolio when someone wants to get their money out." For students or advisers who want to start an investment club but aren't up to taking on all the intricacies of a partnership, a traveling club is the way to go.

Not all student investing clubs restrict themselves to paper portfolios or online contests. We've already mentioned some that invest real money, and if a group of kids and an adult adviser are willing to undertake some of the extra work required to make such a club successful, it can be hugely rewarding. "You take it more seriously and pay more attention when there's real

> **>STREET SLANG**
> **CLOSELY HELD**
> Again, we're talking high finance, nothing else. It describes a public company in which most of the stock is held by a small group of shareholders.

NAIC: An Investment Club's Best Friend

BRAND-NEW INVESTMENT CLUBS would be wise to follow the format that the National Association of Investors Corp. (NAIC) has developed over its fifty-year history. The NAIC's structure, materials, and strategies will work equally well whether you choose to invest via a paper portfolio or by using real money. The group's philosophy is to encourage long-term, sensible investing in growth companies.

NAIC has a wealth of resources for investment clubs—not surprising, since some 37,000 investment clubs are members of the association. Its book, *Starting and Running a Profitable Investment Club* (Times Books, 1996, $15), is the classic reference on how best to organize a club. The association's Stock Selection Guide and club accounting software are invaluable if you're starting a club. In addition NAIC also has local councils staffed by volunteers who can provide support and answer questions you may have.

NAIC has a youth membership for kids ages eighteen and younger. Basic membership costs $20 and includes the association's magazine, *Better Investing*; its youth newsletter; and a membership guide that explains the association's products and services. A deluxe membership cost $45 and includes everything listed above as well as a self-study investor's guide, a mutual fund handbook, a baseball cap, and a stock-reading ruler.

For more information, you can write or call NAIC:

> 711 W. Thirteen Mile Road
> Madison Heights, MI 48071
> 248-583-6242
> www.better-investing.org

money at stake," says Joel Miles, one of the members of the St. George's Junior Investment Club.

The students at Naperville Central High School, under the direction of Kaye Corrigan, have been putting their own money into stocks since the club began in 1994. The Wall $treet Society, as they dubbed their group, meets twice a month from 7 to 8:30 in the evening. The club is so popular that membership has to be limited. In order to keep the club to a manageable size, Corrigan restricts the group to about twenty members. "If there are too many kids, they can get too far removed from it," she says. "We want everyone to be an active player and a participant. Our goal is to involve all the kids; it's not just to throw your money in and make some more money." Members are chosen after going through an interview with the club; a member who misses a lot of meetings is asked to leave the club. "It's not fair for kids to be skipping meetings while we're turning kids away," says Corrigan.

To start in the club, a member contributes $30; the monthly suggested contribution is $15. "You can put in more than that, in increments of $5, but you can't exceed $30 a month," says Corrigan. Currently the group's portfolio is worth $17,350. At every meeting members get a valuation statement indicating how the portfolio is doing and how much their share is worth.

When the group first organized, Corrigan held a parent information meeting. "We told them that we can't guarantee success; we're here to learn and to make our learning a little more successful," she says. "Legally the investment is the parent's. However, the students are making the decisions."

At meetings the club typically divides into research teams of four to five kids to brainstorm about stock ideas. "When we narrow down our choices, we look at *Value Line's* information on the companies, at the NAIC's stock selection guides, at the company's annual reports, and at news reports off the Internet," Corrigan says. "The kids chart the stock price for the last five years and make a presentation. The groups then each recommend one stock to the whole club, and we vote. The students get to vote according to their share of ownership." That means that seniors, who have been contributing to the portfolio for longer, have a greater vote than new members. That way the kids with the most experience—and the most at risk financial-ly—get a larger voting share.

The club has had speakers in to visit ("We interviewed the Beardstown Ladies for a local cable television show," says Corrigan), and they've attended the annual meetings of local companies they own stock in. "One of the companies we used to own was Federal Signal, and Jim Lovell from Apollo 13 was on their board of directors, so the kids got to meet him," she says.

The Wall $treet Society's performance has been strong: annu-alized returns over five years have averaged 33 percent a year. Compare that with the return of the S&P 500 over a similar time period: about 28 percent, a return most professional money managers haven't matched. ("But we tell the kids it's been a very good market for the last five years," says Corrigan.) Among the club's best stock picks over the years have been Intel, Staples, MCI Worldcom, Lucent Technologies, and Disney. "We've also had our share of dogs," says Corrigan. "The lesson we've learned is research, research, research. We got caught up in the excite-ment of the Internet and a couple of years ago had to decide whether to buy Netscape stock or Spyglass. Neither of the com-panies had been around long enough to let us do much research, but we bought one of them. Unfortunately it was Spyglass. Then there are the ones we researched and decided not to buy. We researched Amgen at $40 a share but we didn't buy it. It's now at $150 a share."

Still, the club has made enough that when last year's seniors graduated, they faced the tough decision of whether to cash out their shares or leave them with the club and become a nonvot-ing member. The kids who cashed out received about $1,200, enough, in some cases, to buy a computer to take to college.

Buy, Sell, or Hold: Trouble or Opportunity?

BACK IN 1997, the Naperville High School Investment Club in Naperville, Illinois, had recently bought stock in Columbia/HCA Healthcare, a growing hospital chain, when the news broke that the company was under investigation by the federal government for overbilling Medicare millions of dollars. The club held an emergency summer meeting to determine what it should do with the stock. The firm was the country's largest hospital chain, doing record business. Perhaps this was an isolated incident, and the company and its stock price would recover. Or maybe this investigation was only the beginning of the firm's problems. **Should the club sell, hold, or use this chance to buy even more of the stock?**

What they did: Club members voted to sell the Columbia/HCA Healthcare stock, and by doing so they kept their portfolio healthy. The investigations continued and expanded; the firm's chief executive officer and president were forced to resign, and the stock dropped to about 33. Naperville got out early enough that it sold at 40; the club broke even, which is more than many investors did. The club's decision was based more on instinct than on a complete knowledge of how deep the problem would go. That sort of information simply wasn't available at the time. But it was the same action some professional investors might have taken. Money manager James J. Cramer never hesitates to sell when there is a whiff of financial scandal. "My rule is simple: companies nailed or fessing up to accounting irregularities can't be owned," Cramer says. "Many never come back. Don't try to rationalize, just take the loss and get out."

Buy, Sell, or Hold: Debating a Portfolio's Big Winner

THE ST. GEORGE'S JUNIOR INVESTMENT CLUB had a nice ride with America Online. It was one of the first stock picks the group made when they organized in 1996, and by the spring of 1999 it had split several times and hit a stock price upward of 145. The club's average cost per share of its AOL stock: $3.75. AOL comprised about 45 percent of the club's portfolio and was its big winner. So when the stock dropped below 100 in the summer, it sparked some discussion among club members. **Was the stock going to keep falling? Was now a good time to lock in their gains and sell AOL?**

What they did: The Junior Investment Club members decided to hold on to their AOL stock. In very short order, the club was glad it did. The stock was volatile through the summer of 1999 but steadily climbed back toward 140 through the fall. Another AOL stock split was announced, vindicating the club's faith in the stock. In January 2000, AOL stunned the investment community when it announced it was acquiring Time Warner. It remains to be seen what will happen to the stock price after the deal is complete.

If you're interested in investment clubs, school is not the only venue open to you. We've already heard about the St. George's Junior Investment Club, in Washington, D.C., which was organized through that church. The Mutual Investment Club of Pueblo, Colorado, has four teenage members and about a half-dozen adult members. Some of the kids are the children of adult members, but one joined without a parent. All make the same required contribution that adult members make—between $30 and $50 a month—and all do research and present stock ideas to the group. "The kids are full voting members," says Mike Stapleton, a club leader.

Stapleton's sixteen-year-old son, Chad, is one of the teen members. "The kids in the club pay their dues from money they have from mowing lawns and things like that," Chad says. "I had some money in a savings account that I've been putting into the investment club. I joined mostly because I wanted to make some money, but I also knew it would help me in the future. I had also seen a couple of movies like *Wall Street,* and had an interest." One of the underage members was the impetus behind a new club policy: if a stock that hits a new high declines 25 percent from that high, the group sells the stock. That strategy, Mike says, is to avoid the problem the club has had of holding on to losing stocks too long.

One dilemma clubs face when students invest real money is that not too far down the line the students will graduate and perhaps move away from home. What happens to their shares in the investment club then?

There must be a mechanism for participants to take their money out at any point, in case they move or decide to leave the club. But some graduating students might like to let their money continue to grow with the club. "When high school students graduate, they could leave their money," says Jerry Cooper, a teacher at Burnsville High School in Burnsville, Minnesota, who has served as an adviser to several start-up teen investment clubs. "The club then mails them a monthly valuation to let them know what's going on. My experience is that it's best that if they've graduated they don't put any more money in, but they can leave it in and see what happens over time. If they move, lose interest, or leave the club, the club can see what their valuation is and either pay them the full amount or charge a surrender charge of perhaps 3 percent to cover the administrative costs of taking money out."

More Tips on Starting Your Own Student Investment Club

>>**Look for an adviser.** A teacher in your school would be ideal; in some schools economics teachers, math teachers, or business teachers serve as advisers, although we've also encountered schools where the club was ably led by the school media center director, computer sciences teacher, or social studies teacher. Talk to your school principal or a guidance counselor for suggestions if there isn't an easily identifiable prospect. A parent who has an interest in and a knowledge of investing can also be a good resource and coleader for the club.

>>**Hook up with NAIC** (see above) **and call your local NAIC council for advice.** Their members may be able to tell you whether there are other teen clubs in your area; you could get together to compare portfolios.

>>**Check out the NAIC Web site (www.better-investing.org) and a site called Investment Club Central (www.iclub central.com).** Both sites have a wealth of information about investment clubs, as well as interesting online chats and bulletin boards.

>>**Decide whether you're going to invest real money or use the traveling club format**—either can be fun and enlightening.

>>**If your members are new to the stock market, plan to spend the first couple of months learning the ropes before you start making stock picks.**

>>**Arrange to meet at least twice a month.** If you meet less frequently it will be tough to keep things going. "Many adult

And then there are also some college investment clubs that function almost like professional money managers, investing real money—but not the students' own money. The cash comes from clubs meet once a month, but kids need to keep in contact with this more regularly," says Minnesota investment-club adviser Jerry Cooper. Adds veteran club adviser Beth Hamm, "I'd suggest meeting every other week—the school year is so short anyway."

>>**If you're meeting at school, arrange to have access to the computer lab so you can make use of the vast Internet investing resources.** We'll be talking more about that in Chapter 10.

>>**Consider meeting on a weekday evening or a Saturday morning.** One of the biggest obstacles clubs report is meeting conflicts with after-school sports and activities.

>>**Consider holding an Investors' Fair to show other students and parents what the club does.** It will help convince parents of the value of what you're doing and help in recruiting new student members. "Our Investors' Fair is a time for the kids to shine," says Cooper. "They can demonstrate on a computer how the software to study a stock works, or prepare charts of the various stocks they have bought. Maybe if the club owns stock in a local company, that company could send a speaker."

>>**Keep it fun.** Take some of the suggestions offered by clubs in this chapter. Visit an annual meeting of a local company (call the investor relations person ahead of time—you may be able to arrange a special tour). If you're located near a city with a stock exchange, arrange a field trip; otherwise a visit to a local brokerage firm can be interesting. NAIC periodically has seminars and Investors' Fairs that you could arrange to visit.

foundations and groups committed to giving would-be investors some practice. The kids in these groups learn that there's a difference between studying investing and really doing it.

Is Your Money Old Money or New Money?

IF YOU'VE EVER RECEIVED an "old" dollar bill that is worn or ripped, you know that paper currency doesn't last forever. Every year the Bureau of Engraving and Printing takes bills out of circulation due to their poor condition. In fact, about 95 percent of the 37 million notes (bills of every denomination) printed each day are used to replace notes already in circulation.

How long does a piece of paper currency last? It depends on how gently it has been handled. The Bureau estimates that a piece of currency can be folded 4,000 times (first forward and then backward) before it will tear. And, it's not surprising that the lower the denomination, the shorter the life span. After all, a one-dollar bill is passed around from wallet to cash register and back to someone's wallet more frequently than a one hundred dollar bill. Below are the average life spans of notes, as estimated by the Federal Reserve.

$1	18 months
$5	2 years
$10	3 years
$20	4 years
$50	9 years
$100	9 years

The DePauw Investment Alliance, at DePauw University in Greencastle, Indiana, in September 1999 began investing a $60,000 fund that had been sitting semidormant. "It was donated decades ago for the purpose of starting a student investment club," says twenty-year-old sophomore and club president Kirsten Hagen, "but it hadn't been touched in years." Many of the thirty students are business majors; several are in a particular investment analysis course at the school. At this writing, the new investment club is debating how to shape the portfolio. One winner already in the portfolio is Lucent Technologies, a descendant of the AT&T stock that was bought years ago.

The Mount Union College investment team in Alliance, Ohio, manages three different portfolios, which have different investment objectives. The conservative portfolio, donated by the Hillier Foundation for the purpose of giving students experience in investing, is currently worth some $93,000. Another portfolio—aggressively managed and part of a college investment team contest run by Oak Associates, an Ohio money management firm—is worth about $170,000, and the third student portfolio, endowed by the college itself and with a moderately aggressive investment mandate, is worth about $50,000. "The students have to submit an application and a letter saying why they want to be on the team," says Patricia Matthews, the group's adviser and a professor at Mount Union. "They don't have to be a finance major, but they have to have the time and dedication to do this. The kids meet once or maybe twice a week during the school year, and then during the summer we try to meet once or twice a month." Carla Di Salvatore, a twenty-one-year-old accounting and business major, says that her experience with the group has been invaluable. "I had a basic grasp of the market," she says, "but I hadn't done any investing on my own. The biggest thing has just been learning how to evaluate a company and to know what to look for in its financial statements, in the

> **>STREET SLANG**
>
> **OTC**
> **Stands for "over-the-counter"
> stocks which aren't traded on an
> exchange.** Usually these are small
> or start-up companies that can't
> meet the requirements of the
> exchanges for listing. OTC stocks
> make for risky investments,
> since dependable information
> is much harder to come by for
> these stocks.

news, and in the charts." Di Salvatore plans to invest as soon as she's out of school and earning a salary. Mike Holdford, a twenty-one-year-old student from Youngstown, Ohio, had done a little investing before he joined the group. "In high school the bank my dad worked for had an IPO, and I bought shares," he says. "I got it at $10 a share; they had a capital distribution of $6 a share, and it's now back up to $9." But the investment group has given him practice. "Controlling a portfolio is a great experience," says Holdford. "You learn a lot from your mistakes and also from your gains."

ONLINE INVESTMENT CLUBS

SOME KIDS USE THE INTERNET FOR MORE THAN JUST research: they belong to an online investment club. These clubs operate much the same way regular clubs do, collecting money each month from each member, requiring each member to research stocks, and voting on which stocks the club will buy with its money. The main difference is in time and geography. Because the clubs communicate via e-mail and online bulletin boards rather than having a set meeting time, online investment clubs can include members who live in different time zones and who have constantly changing schedules.

The same legal prohibitions to underage investing apply in online clubs as in other types of investment clubs. Accounts must be in a parent's or other custodian's name.

"Come, Watson, come!
The game is afoot!"

SIR ARTHUR CONAN DOYLE IN
THE RETURN OF SHERLOCK HOLMES

Trading Games

ARE YOU EAGER TO TRY YOUR HAND AT TRADING stocks? Do you think that maybe you have the secret to making big money in the market? There's a way you can flex your muscles and trade stocks to your heart's content, a place where you can try every investment theory you've read about or heard about and buy and sell every stock you've seen mentioned in chat rooms. Every time you read about a stock and think, "If I had the money, I'd invest in. . .," you can.

All this trading won't cost you a penny. And although you don't get to take home the profits from your investing, if you're very lucky or very smart—or both—you might win some prizes, perhaps even some cash. At the very least, you will experience investing in a way that's as close to reality as you can get. I'm talking about stock market simulation games and contests, which seem to be all over the Internet these days.

The basic concept of these games is that you have a hypothetical grubstake, say $100,000 or $500,000, to invest. You can either buy and hold your "paper portfolio" of securities—nowadays, "virtual portfolio" is more like it—or you can buy and sell stocks throughout the duration of the competition, usually anywhere between one and three months.

Teens and young investors love competing in these games. "Our national public contest is open to anyone," says Sam Polk of Virtual Stock Exchange. "We regularly have a stunning number of college students in the top twenty winners."

Young investors have different motives for jumping in. For Vijay Saluja, an eighteen-year-old prodigy from Michigan (he simultaneously completed his high school and college degrees), who won first in The Investment Challenge (an Internet-based game with cash prizes) for two consecutive semesters, playing the game was a way to try his hand at the market. "It seemed like something fun to do," he says. "I didn't have money to invest at the time, but I was always telling my dad about stocks I wanted to buy, and then I'd see those stocks go up. I thought it would be a good experience to see how well I could do."

The best known of these games is the Stock Market Game, which is distributed and organized by the Securities Industry Association's education arm, the Securities Industry Foundation for Economic Education (SIFEE). This game, which was started back in 1977, is played mostly in schools in grades four through twelve. (College and adult versions of the game are also available.) When the Stock Market Game began, it was played on paper. Kids and their teachers (teachers have to go through training sessions before they can run a game) had the laborious exercise of filling out stock selection sheets and mailing them in to be processed. They then had to wait to see—days later, via return mail—whether their buy and sell orders had been executed the way they wanted. While the paper game is still available to schools that don't have Web access, the Internet version of the game, Stock Market Game Worldwide, is far easier to use. Kids can enter their orders via their classroom computers and check their portfolios daily.

Not surprisingly, the Stock Market Game's popularity has grown quickly. In 1999, more than 700,000 kids played the game nationally; which is an increase of 80 percent over the past ten years. The coordinators around the country expect the game to grow tremendously over the next several years, as Internet access becomes routine in schools. In summer 1999, SIFEE upgraded the capacity of the Stock Market Game's computer system; the previous spring the Web site had been receiving a million hits a day. In addition, the Stock Market Game has gone international; students in fifteen countries now play, trading on the U.S. stock markets. For the most part, according to a spokesperson, those players are kids in English-speaking and international schools.

The Stock Market Game is run within each state by a coordinator, and the rules and prizes vary slightly. (Some states require more diversification in a portfolio than other states do.) To find out the specifics of your state's program, go to the general Web site (**www.smgww.org**) to locate your state's Web site. One of the strengths of the Stock Market Game is that the classroom teachers who lead a game must be trained by game organizers. This insures the game leader is knowledgeable and qualified.

Although it's the largest and best known, the Stock Market Game isn't the only game in town. The Internet has made running and distributing these games easy, and literally dozens are available on finance-oriented Web sites. (For a listing of games, see "Are You Game?" on the following page.)

Why so many games? Web sites offer them, sometimes for free, to attract visitors to their site so they can sell advertising. They're sponsored by brokerage firms, financial magazines, financial news sites, and so on. "I first heard about investing contests through E*Trade," says Chris Stallman, a sixteen-year-

Are You Game?

BELOW IS CONTACT INFORMATION for some of the better-known kid-oriented stock market games and simulations. Details on specific games—such as contest starting and ending periods, prizes, and rules and entry fees—change so frequently that the best way to get up-to-the minute info is to check out the games' Web sites. Overall descriptions will be available on the *Street Wise* Web site, too (www.streetwise teen.com). Ladies and gentlemen, start your portfolios!

The Stock Market Game	**www.smgww.org**
Investment Challenge	**www.ichallenge.net**
MainXchange	**www.mainxchange.com**
CNBC Student Stock Tournament	**www.sst.cnbc.com**
Salomon Smith Barney Young Investors Network Portfolio Contest	**www.salomonsmithbarney.com**
Virtual Stock Exchange	**www.virtualstockexchange.com**
Stock-Trak Portfolio Simulations	**www.stocktrak.com**

old investor who has his own investment newsletter. "I decided to get into it to see how I would do against lots of other people. Later I heard about more contests and began entering them. I've tried Yahoo's Investment Challenge, E*Trade's Stocks game, E*Trade's Stocks and Options game, Marketplayer.com, and Nordby's contest." A casual search by this writer turned up even more games and contests on sites such as TheStreet.com, Fortune.com, Forbes.com, and America Online.

On many of these, the rules state that you must be over eighteen to play. Some kids get around this by having a parent register and playing the game under the parent's name, or by just signing on as adults when they're not. For all practical purposes, what those age limits mean is that is you have to be over eighteen to be awarded the prizes. "We operate our promotions and games in accordance with what we understand state and federal regulations to be, and this is one of them," said a Yahoo spokesperson when asked why kids under the age of eighteen can't play. "Prizes only go to qualified winners, and an individual under the age of eighteen would not be considered qualified."

But never fear: there is no shortage of games designed especially for kids. **Investment Challenge (www.ichallenge.net)** runs fall- and spring-semester contests that last eight to nine weeks and can be played by individuals as well as classroom groups. **CNBC**, the cable television financial news network, sponsors classroom games (**www.sst.cnbc.com**). **MainXchange**'s (**www. mainxchange.com**) game is geared to both classroom teams and individuals. **Virtual Stock Exchange (www.virtualstockexchange.com**), which has the capacity for classroom competitions and also individual contests and allows players of all ages, says that 14 percent of its competitors are under age 17. **Salomon Smith Barney's Young Investors Network (www.salomonsmithbarney.com**) has a pilot contest played in schools, and the brokerage house is planning to expand it.

There are even local contests, which, because they attract a smaller pool of contestants, may be easier to win. For example, a Philadelphia money management firm, Roffman Miller Associates, runs a contest at a Philadelphia center-city school every year. The winner gets $1,100 toward college.

Which brings us to the subject of prizes. Some of these contests have great prizes, ranging from designer clothes to cash (always in fashion) to airline tickets to real stocks. Last year, the first-prize winner of Investment Challenge took home $2,000.

The CNBC winners get 200 shares of General Electric stock (recent value: more than $20,000). Virtual Stock Exchange winners get cash prizes, although smaller than those awarded in some other competitions: the top three winners get $300, $200, and $100. MainXchange winners get merchandise from the Web site's sponsors. Recent prizes included clothing from Nautica and Tommy Hilfiger, a computer, software, and even airline tickets. Winners in the Salomon Smith Barney game get a share each of Citigroup stock, worth $52 at this writing.

An unexpected consequence of winning some of these games has been the notoriety and respect it has brought to the kids. In spring 1999, the winning team in CNBC's Student Stock Tournament consisted of three sixteen-year-old girls from Baraboo, Wisconsin. Casey Fox, Brienne Newman, and Colleen Zophy knew they were ranked in the top five in the contest, but they didn't realize they had finished first until CNBC anchor Bill Griffeth came to their school to do a live television spot with them on CNBC. "Our teacher knew about two weeks ahead of time, and he sent a letter to our parents, but they kept it a secret," says Newman. "There were TV crews everywhere. It was exciting."

Even when the winners haven't been on national television, they've gained guru status in their schools and with friends. "People ask for stock tips now," says Preetam Bagalkotkar of Langley, Virginia, a second-place winner in Investment Challenge. "An assistant principal in my school came up to me and asked me if some teachers all pitched in money together, would I manage it for them? He wasn't joking. I told him, 'Let's wait a while for that.'" Bagalkotkar is smart; there can be legal ramifications when you start managing money for other people.

The rules of investing competitions vary from game to game. Some, like the CNBC game, are more conservative and don't allow trading on margin, options trading, or short selling. Some games don't even allow any trading during the contest, requiring kids to buy their stocks at the beginning of the game and hold them until the end. And others provide students with a list of stocks they must choose from. Other common restrictions in stock market simulations involve not letting an investor buy stocks that sell for less than a certain price, say $1 or $3 a share. That's to prevent kids from buying the volatile and easily manipulated penny stocks. In others, such as the freewheeling Investment Challenge game, anything (or almost anything) goes: options, short selling, buying on margin.

How close do these contests come to replicating the actual experience of trading stocks? About as close as you can within the framework of a contest. Of course, nothing can mimic how you feel when you've lost a chunk of money in the stock market, but players report that they definitely get swept up in the competition and that emotions do play a part. "In the beginning of the game, I wasn't counting on getting one of the top places," says Alec Hufnagel, age fifteen, an Investment Challenge veteran (and third-place winner in its spring 1999 contest). "But once I started doing well and there was a chance I could get a prize, I was checking my stocks all the time. During the last week, it seemed like I checked them every half hour. If my stocks did well, I was overjoyed, and if they went down, I felt like I was having a down day." Vijay Saluja, the eighteen-year-old who won the Investment Challenge twice, reports that he, too, felt the pressure build as the games went on. "Even though it's not real money, it felt like I had $2,000 at risk, because that was the prize," he says.

Complaints about the games vary. "I tried a contest," says eighteen-year-old high school senior Jason Orlovsky, "but it frustrated me. In the game I joined, I couldn't use limit orders to control what price I bought at. I'd put through an order to buy a stock that was selling for a certain price, and by the time the order was executed, the price was $20 a share higher." Orlovsky prefers to concentrate on his real-life investments.

Kids have found that these games have their share of glitch-

Why Real Life is Different

ANYONE WHO HAS EVER RUN a paper portfolio has wondered whether a successful performance could be duplicated in real life. Usually not. Here are a couple of the reasons why.

1. Games often allow you to trade huge chunks of a company's stock. In real life, buying and selling that many shares would move the market, and you wouldn't be able to trade at the prices you'd like.

2. Trading with real bucks introduces two emotional aspects that are often missing from the games: fear and greed. Because nobody wants to lose real money, there's the sensible temptation to take less risk. Think about it: if you had managed to turn $100,000 into $250,000 in the space of five or six weeks in real life, wouldn't you want to cash out at least some of that to lock in your returns? But cashing out would prevent you from doubling your stake again. It's that old risk-and-reward correlation again: less risk means that the rewards, even if they come, almost certainly aren't quite as big.

3. Taxes. Few games take capital gains taxes into account, because to do so would be an accounting nightmare. In real life, the IRS is your ever-present trading partner.

es, some of them caused by mistakes on the kids' part. A team that played the Stock Market Game in New Jersey last year had some typical problems: one student meant to sell 100 shares of a stock, clicked on the wrong button, and bought another 100 shares by mistake. Another team member put through an order to buy GAP stock, thinking it was the hip retailer. Unfortunately, GAP is the ticker symbol for Great Atlantic and Pacific Tea Company, better known as the A&P supermarket chain. (The Gap trades under the symbol GPS.) Some of the technical problems are due to Web site traffic jams, which sponsors report they're trying to fix. But it's a safe bet there will always be glitches.

Many game sponsors have addressed another gripe that players have had in the past: the use of delayed stock quotes. "I like using real-time quotes," says Saluja. "Delayed quotes is the dumbest thing. The Internet stocks can fluctuate $10 in fifteen minutes, so it's kind of pointless to enter an order on delayed quotes. The market can be up all day, then drop 20 percent in the last fifteen minutes."

And kids should be aware that some games cost money to enter. Investment Challenges charges a $30 registration fee, for example, and fees for the Stock Market Game vary according to state, ranging from $5 to $25 (although sometimes local sponsors or school boards will pick up the cost for student teams).

Adults have different reservations about these games and the lessons kids are taking away from them. Jeffrey Fox, head of the young investor program at the National Association of Investors Corp., is uncomfortable with the sums kids play with in investing contests. "Kids get used to investing $100,000 in fake money and think that's how much they need to begin investing," he says. "They're not getting the idea of putting $25 or $50 a month into the market for the long term." Another complaint is that most games don't allow you to invest in mutual funds, which are the cornerstone of many a long-term financial plan.

Grown-ups also worry that game playing encourages too much speculation and short-term trading. "The whole purpose of the game is to introduce kids to the basic concepts of economic education," says Donna Haggarty of SIFEE. "We hope that in addition to teaching math, the game teaches something about social studies and geography. We also hope they enjoy the opportunity to experience what financial risk is like without spending any money. We're not trying to turn people into day traders or little Gordon Gekkos (Gordon Gekko is the fictional character at the center of the movie *Wall Street*. Gekko's signature line: "Greed is good.")

Teachers and adults who deal with the kids playing the games say that for the most part, kids know the difference between the stock market games and real-life trading. "Kids definitely get it," says William Wood, an economics professor at James Madison University in Virginia. "I know teachers who use the example of a race car driver. Someone like Jeff Gordon, the champion driver, may go 180 miles an hour on the racetrack, but he doesn't drive like that when he gets in his car to go to the store. The same thing is true of these games."

If anything, sometimes an experience with a stock market game can convince a novice investor not to take big risks. Matt Hooker, age twenty, is a finance major at Notre Dame in South Bend, Indiana, who first started investing when he was fifteen. "I played the Stock-Trak game through an organization at school. I was trying to time the market with eBay and Amazon. I watched them go up and up and thought, 'You've got to be kidding me; they're so overvalued,' but they kept going up. So I thought I'd just try to get in. At the point I got in, they had a correction, and they were my worst investments. I bought Amazon I think at 150, and it went to 90, and that's when the game ended. It definitely turned me away from ever wanting to day trade or time the market."

That echoes what contest-playing kids say about their real money investments. "I have a couple of real stocks," says Alec Hufnagel, the Investment Challenge top-three finisher, "but I have them for the long term. I own Microsoft and AT&T, blue chips mostly. Real-life investing is totally different. I would never trade options in real life. You can gain or lose 50 percent of your money in hours. It's way too nerve-wracking with real money."

HOW TO WIN: STRATEGIES FOR STOCK SIMULATION GAMES

WHEN YOU PLAY A STOCK MARKET SIMULATION GAME, THERE are two ways you can go. You can:

(a) follow the guidelines you've learned for investing for a lifetime, diversifying prudently, and not taking too much risk. This can be a great way to use these games to try your hand at investing. You can compare your performance to different market indices and see how you've done against the S&P 500, for instance, or compare your performance to that of friends and classmates. Or you can:

(b) go for broke. This is your best shot to actually win.

The truth about stock market simulation games, and the reason that some adults who are concerned about economic education are troubled by some games, is that to win you need to forget all the lessons you've learned about smart long-term investing. Rather than choosing several stocks in different industries (to spread the risk that any one industry will falter) and stocks that they think will rise in value over the long term, contest winners have tended to make big bets on one or two stocks. "The truth is that if you put together a solid, diversified portfolio, you have zero chance to win these contests," says Lewis Mandell, dean of the School of Management at the State University of New York–Buffalo. "You have nothing to lose in these games, so you take the greatest possible risk position."

First of all, remember that the time frame for these games is nearly always weeks, not years or even months. That's because most games are designed to fit into a semester or part of a semester. Participants have to ask themselves whether they think a stock is going up in the next four or eight or ten weeks, not in a year or two.

And as Mandell mentioned above, unlike in real-money

Buy, Sell, or Hold: Investing Their Prize Money

WHEN A TEAM OF THREE SOPHOMORE GIRLS at Baraboo High School in Baraboo, Wisconsin, won first place in a CNBC Student Stock Tournament in 1999, they were awarded General Electric stock (GE owns CNBC) worth about $20,000. It was decided that the award would go into a school scholarship fund. The girls themselves are slated to be the first recipients of the fund; in the meantime they are acting as the fund's investment officers.

An agreement with the school decrees that the money, which is held in a trust, is invested 50 percent in equities, 25 percent in cash, and 25 percent in a mutual fund. (The girls have chosen Fidelity's Blue Chip mutual fund.) The girls decided for now to keep half of the equity money in GE stock, and they bought stock in 4 Kids Entertainment (KIDE) with the other half. 4 Kids, the toy company that licenses the hot Pokemon toys, is the stock that took the team to the CNBC win. By the time the trust was set up and all the legalities taken care of, the girls bought 4 Kids at 52. Within two weeks it had shot up to 85, but then the stock began to drop.

investing, there's nothing to lose by betting big. "In a local game near here," says William Wood, "the winners of the game are recognized at a luncheon. If you make a big bet and win, you go to the luncheon. If you only match the market, you will lose and not go to the luncheon, and if you bet big and lose, you don't go, either. So the result is the same whether you match the market or lose your shirt." Why not take a flier?

That's what a team of students at Brinley Middle School in Las Vegas did last year in the Stock Market Game. Guided by teacher Kimberly Hardgrove, the team took their hypothetical

Should they continue holding or cash out and take their profits?

What they did: At the suggestion of the local stockbroker who handles the trades for the trust, the girls entered a stop order on it so the stock would be sold automatically if it dipped to a certain level. The price they chose for the stop order: 72, which would still represent a nice profit over the 52 they bought the stock at.

"The girls wanted to protect some of the profit they made," says Baraboo High math teacher and investment club adviser Chris Labeots. "They also decided that they would buy it back at 60 if it dropped that far." Shortly after they placed the stop order, the stock price did indeed drop, opening on the next trading day at 66 11/16. The Baraboo team's stock was sold. Later that day the stock climbed back above 73, but the team was still gratified to know they'd made a 38 percent profit (not counting commission costs) over a few weeks.

$100,000 portfolio and bought a single stock, Ameritrade, using margin to increase their leverage. (If you have a stock that's a winner, buying on margin can boost your returns dramatically.) That strategy worked brilliantly. By the end of the eleven-week contest, the portfolio had a market value of $907,023, and the kids were crowned winners. (Hardgrove's class also successfully participated in a MainXchange contest last spring.)

Some games now require contestants to hold at least three or five stocks in a portfolio to encourage some diversification. That's a good idea, but the fact remains that to win big, you need

Be Careful!

ALTHOUGH IT'S FUN TO PLAY stock market games via the Internet, watch out for Web sites that take you, after a few clicks, to a real trading and investing function. It's easy to see how you might believe you're playing a game when you're actually entering stock trades.

A game should never request a Social Security number or other personal financial identification from you, while setting up a real investing account would require that sort of identification. If a game charges to play (remember there are plenty that are free!), you will have to give a credit card number, but never a Social Security number. Even asking for a credit card number should raise a red flag, and alert you to examine the Web site carefully. This is definitely a time to call in mom or dad to have a look and not merely to borrow a credit card from them!

to be loaded up heavily on a big performing stock.

Another strategy, in the games that allow it, is to trade options. All three of the top winners in Investment Challenge's 1999 spring-semester game used options to pump up their portfolios. Vijay Saluja, the first-place winner in the fall and spring 1998–1999 games, credits the game with teaching him about options. Alec Hufnagel, who placed third in the national challenge, had some buddies who quickly brought him up to speed on playing to win. "I had two friends who came in second in an earlier competition explain how options worked," says Hufnagel. "By the second day of the contest, I had already purchased five options." Second-place winner Preetam Bagalkotkar, whose older brother (who happens to be a physician) clued him in on the advantages of options, actually abandoned buying regular stock shares altogether. "I started out buying shares, but my brother told me that options are the better way to make money," he says. "Now I know about options, and I don't buy shares anymore in the games." Bagalkotkar ran his $500,000 portfolio stake into $1.6 million by the game's end.

Regardless of what you think of momentum investing as a long-term investment strategy, several investment contest winners and their teachers swear by it. Momentum investing says that you should buy stocks with a recent history of rising prices (the idea being that these stocks are already moving up and will keep up their momentum for a while). It's akin to jumping on a bandwagon. Contest winners need stocks that are going somewhere fast, and if they can hop on a hot stock that everyone's talking about, it may go places faster than an obscure, undervalued stock.

Holding cash is never a good idea in stock market simulation contests. Some games don't credit you with any return on cash in your portfolio, and even games that give some sort of return on a cash balance usually use a low-money-market sort of interest rate. A couple of percentage points' worth of return isn't going to get you to any awards luncheons.

Another tip, which contests tell you but players may misunderstand: at the end of the game, don't sell your portfolio. If you do you'll incur the trading commissions that many games build into their programs. Instead, let your portfolio freeze at the ending date, and the game organizer will just note its market value.

With games that have thousands of participants—or hundreds of thousands, in the case of some of the national Internet games for adult investors—it takes more than a smart investor to win. It takes a large dollop of luck, too. So keep your accomplishments in perspective. If you match or beat the market over the course of the game, you should be proud of yourself, regardless of where you place. After all, many professional money managers would love to be able to say they consistently beat the market.

Good luck!

"Information about money has become almost as important as money itself."

WALTER WRISTON, FORMER
CHAIRMAN OF CITIBANK

10

Navigating the Internet and Other Resources

INTERNET

ISN'T THE TWENTY-FIRST CENTURY GRAND? YOU ARE living in a golden age for individual investors. Information is power, and through the Internet, you have access to more information at a lower price than ever before in history.

What makes the Internet so ideal for kids? It's a combination of a couple of things. "There's a classic cartoon from *The New Yorker* where the caption is 'On the Internet no one knows you're a dog,'" says Douglas Gerlach, founder of the Invest-orama Web site (**www.investorama.com**) and author of *The Complete Idiot's Guide to Online Investing.* "On the Internet, no one knows you're a teenager; you're just another person online. It's perfect for people who are just getting started. There are places where you can go and ask questions where you don't feel intimidated. On the Internet you can ask the questions and you may feel a little dumb, but nobody knows you."

Another factor is something you know already: teens are wired. A recent CBS News/*New York Times* poll of thirteen-to-seventeen-year-olds found that 63 percent of them regularly use a computer at home and 48 percent regularly go online at home. And that's not even counting the kids who have access through school computers.

But the big bonus of the Internet for both teen and adult investors is the sheer volume of business information that's available. Much of the information on the Net is free (once you have basic Internet access). Ten years ago it was a big deal to get even twenty-minute-delayed stock quotes. Investors would drop in at their local brokerage office during lunch hour to check stock quotes or buy special devices and subscribe to special services just to get quotes. Now they're free for the taking on most financial Web sites. "When I started investing in the 1990s," says Gerlach, "I spent one Saturday a month at the public library reading S&P reports. I remember standing in line to get *Value Line* and the magazines I wanted and dumping dimes into the photocopy machine. Now you get S&P reports for one or two dollars, and many brokers are giving them out for free. Other financial sites have stepped up their resources for financial research. Everything you need to do an analysis of a company is online."

In addition to the corporate and professional Web sites for investors, such as CBS Marketwatch (**www.marketwatch.com**), Bloomberg (**www.bloomberg.com**), and Yahoo's site (**finance. yahoo.com**), some investing-savvy teens have even started their own sites to Web-cast their opinions and insights about the stock market. It's fun to see what other interested kids have to say about investing.

But at the same time, it's important to be aware of the big downside of the Internet. It's easy for someone to distribute false information, either negative or positive, about a stock. The Internet is to a rumor as a petri dish is to bacteria: the perfect medium. There are any number of investing bulletin boards and chat rooms devoted to discussing particular stocks: take what you read there with a very large dose of skepticism. Someone who owns a stock has an incentive to hype it; someone who has sold a stock short has an incentive to try to drive the price down by trashing it. Employees of a company have an obvious motive to pass on damaging information about a competitor. Look to the respected names in financial information for data and news on stocks; they don't have a financial interest in seeing the stock price move.

Below are some sites I have found to be especially interesting or useful. Happy surfing.

SITES ESPECIALLY FOR — AND BY — YOUNG INVESTORS

>>**A. G. Edwards** (**www.agedwards.com/bma/index/shtml**). This brokerage firm's site features "The Big Money Adventure," an educational segment with choose-a-guides that include Gold Bullion (a bull in a superhero costume) and Sell Hi (a robot). There are games to play and print-out coloring pages, both of which might be boring to teens. In fact, "Storybook Adventures" labels itself as being for ages six to ten; "Star Traders" is a stock-picking game (with T-shirts as prizes) that describes itself as being for ages ten to adult.

>>**Buck Investor** (**www.buckinvestor.com**). "Building wealth by bucking the trend" is the motto of this site, which is geared to investors under the age of thirty-five and sports an antlered buck as its mascot. The site has useful articles, bulletin boards, a weekly e-mail newsletter, profiles of young investors, and links to other helpful sites. It was begun by a pair of North

Carolina State students three years ago, and in 1999 they sold it and moved to San Francisco, where they continue to work with the site under the new owner.

>>**Bulls and Bears Club** (**//members.aol.com/fozz148/index. html**). The Palos Verdes Peninsula High School investment club posts this site, which includes favorite Web links and an overview of the club. A great site for kids interested in starting a school club.

>>**BuyandHold.com** (**www.buyandhold.com**). Buyandhold describes itself as an online broker for long-term investors. It has a rock-bottom commission charge: $2.99 per stock trade order. It also allows investors to buy partial shares (ideal for the investor on a budget). This Web site also has a first-rate educational section and a worthwhile Kids & Investing section.

>>**DoughNet** (**www.doughnet.com**). This is an online bank for kids, with a few noticeable differences. You can deposit money and shop at stores that are part of the network's online shopping mall (the money is deducted from your account or, if a parent has given approval, charged to the parent's credit card). You can also donate to charitable causes using your account or your credit line. There is some cursory investing information here, but the emphasis really is on spending at the DoughNet stores. Your time is better spent elsewhere.

>>**Edustock** (**tqd.advanced.org/3088/**). Begun by students at Winston Churchill High School in Potomac, Maryland, this site has simulated market trading as well as basic information on investing and profiles of a group of companies young investors might be interested in. It's bright, well designed, and easy to use.

>>Investing for Kids (tqd.advanced.org//3096). This unique site, done by students at Palos Verdes Peninsula High School in California (the same school as the Bulls and Bears Club, but different kids), has an abundance of information for all levels of teen investors. One feature is the ThinkQuest Stock Game, where you invest a $100,000 cyberportfolio. The investing information is wisely organized according to investing ability (beginner, intermediate, and advanced). This Yahoo! cool site richly deserves the attention.

>>InvestSmart (//library.advanced.org/10326). Another site designed for ThinkQuest, a kid's Web page design competition, this one is well worth bookmarking, with a market simulation, investment lessons, and a more active bulletin board than many other kid investing sites. The "Real Life Examples" make for great reading about how specific kids got started. Yahoo! has also awarded this "cool site" status.

>>Jump$tart Coalition for Financial Literacy (www.jump-startcoalition.org). The Coalition is a clearinghouse, primarily for teachers, for personal finance resources produced by various organizations. Although not targeted to student investors, this can be a great resource if you're looking for materials and information for a school investment club or other in-school investment activities. If you have a teacher who wants to know where to look for more information to pass on to students, this is the site to recommend.

>>Kidstock (www.kidstock.com). Kidstock is attractive and well put together, with articles on how kids can earn money, the basics of investing, and direct stock investing (buying stocks directly from a company). It's part of Netstock Direct, a Web site devoted to direct investing and dividend reinvestment plans.

>>**Moneyopolis** (**www.moneyopolis.org**). In this math-and-money interactive game geared to kids in grades six through eight, kids answer questions and solve math problems as they travel around "Moneyopolis." The accounting firm Ernst & Young created this one.

>>**Motley Fool** (**www.fool.com/familyfool**). Well known to investors of all ages, Motley Fool has a special section for teens and investing, with articles on investing and stock market basics and a teen bulletin board. A great site for all ages.

>>**National Association of Investors Corp. (NAIC)** (**www.better-investing.org**). This site, home to thousands of investment clubs, has a section on youth investing that is full of valuable articles and tips. It should also be the starting place for anyone interested in an investment club.

>>**Savvynews** (**www.savvynews.com**). At this writing this site was still under construction, designed to replace a site called www.MrMarkets.com. The old site, run by Omaha, Nebraska, student Doug Sherrets, included a column written by him and an active message board. The new site bears watching.

>>**Salomon Smith Barney** (**www.smithbarney.com/yin**). The Young Investor Network section of the firm's main Web site is designed to let you run a paper portfolio as well as check out articles on investing. Well organized for the beginning investor.

>>**Stockrebel.com** (**www.stockrebel.com**). Daniel Abrahamson is MrBizWhiz, also known as stockrebel.com, and also known as the "rebel with a portfolio." This Connecticut teen has his own fun, irreverent, and opinionated Web site where he keeps track of his recommended portfolio and posts his analyses of different stocks.

>>**Streetadvisor** (**www.streetadvisor.com**). Not strictly a young investor's site, Streetadvisor is noteworthy because it was founded by a student at Texas Christian University, Kevin Prigel, when he was nineteen years old. This well-executed site contains detailed investment news and analysis, often provided by securities analysts. Streetadvisor covers the technology industry especially well.

>>**StrongKids** (**www.strongkids.com**). Created by Strong Mutual Funds, this site has a standard toolbox for kids and parents interested in investing: an interactive calculator, a library of articles on investing, and information on the company's mutual funds.

>>**Undergraduate Investment News** (**www.uinews.com**). A Harvard economics undergrad started this site, which publishes articles by undergrads from around the country. In addition to investing info, the site often discusses career and academic issues ("Graduate School Timeline").

>>**Wall Street Wizard** (**www.streetwhiz.com**). This site was begun by a seventeen-year-old Californian, Jay Liebowitz, now a student at the University of Pennsylvania's Wharton School. It is heavy with articles on a variety of topics, from information for the newbie to a section on business heroes and villains. Liebowitz has a fun sense of humor and a clear-eyed view of investing. As of late, Liebowitz is only updating the site weekly, due to his college schedule.

>>**YoungBiz.com** (**www.youngbiz.com**). Two money topics of interest to many teens—investing and entrepreneurship—are the focus of this site. Youngbiz has investing info, a weekly spotlight profile of a stock that kids might be interested in, and message boards. CNBC profiled YoungBiz.com as a Powerlunch Cool Site.

>>**Young Investor** (www.younginvestor.com). Fun and well designed, this is a good beginning stop for a young investor. The site is brought to you by the folks at Liberty Mutual's Stein Roe Young Investor mutual fund, so that fund is highlighted. Visitors to the site choose one of six guides, who include super-hero Gnaz Dax, snowboarder Slice, eco-conscious Planet Lisa, and career-focused Webster. Beware when choosing a guide: your guide will greet you whenever you return to the site. (When my son visited, he chose Slice, the snowboarder. Now when he logs onto the site he gets greetings like "Glad you could make it back. OK, dude, let's hit the money slope. You lead.") The site has articles on investing, games, information about the Stein Roe fund holdings, and kid bulletin boards. Older teens may not find it as useful as younger kids.

>>**Young Money** (www.youngmoney.com). This is the Internet site of *Young Money,* a monthly magazine about kids and money. For the most part, the site contains information about the magazine, such as the current issue's table of contents. You'll also find an online loan calculator for figuring car payments.

>>**Young Monthly** (www.youngmonthly.com). Chris Stall-man, a fifteen-year-old Chicago-area student, started this attractive site in 1999. Among its unique features is its "Young 30" stock index, which tracks the performance of thirty companies of interest to young investors (for instance, Abercrombie & Fitch, Charles Schwab, AT&T, General Mills, and Wal-Mart).

GENERAL INVESTING SITES

MANY OF THE TOP INVESTOR SITES AREN'T AIMED SPECIFICAL-ly at kids, but that doesn't mean you can't profit from them. In fact, as you become more knowledgeable and sophisticated about investing, you'll find you rely more on sites like the ones below, rather than the educational sites, for data to use in making investment decisions. Most have stock quotes and can be personalized to some degree, typically with a sample portfolio that will pop up with updated prices when you visit. Most of these sites also display basic data like recent financial headlines and the last reported position of market indices, such as the Dow Industrial Average and the S&P 500.

>>**CBS Marketwatch** (**www.marketwatch.com**). The site offers well-written features, breaking news, and good basic research information on companies and stocks, as well as the fairly standard interactive features such as a stock screener, lists of stocks that analysts have upgraded or downgraded, and stocks that have hit fifty-two-week highs and lows. Marketwatch is also home to several columnists worth reading.

>>**CyberInvest** (**www.cyberinvest.com**). This multipurpose supersite has free information on every investing topic imaginable. One of the coolest areas compares the features offered by different financially oriented sites—the financial magazine sites, the investing supersites, and online news sites. It provides a nice snapshot of the Web's financial world.

>>**Dismal Scientist** (**www.dismal.com**). Named after what Thomas Carlyle dubbed economics ("a dismal science"), this site is interesting, although not immediately useful for investors. Click here to read articles like "The Top Twenty-Five Economic Events of the Twentieth Century" and to increase your general economic knowledge, not to get stock-picking ideas.

>>**FinanCenter** (**www.financenter.com**). This site offers one-stop shopping for financial calculations. You pick a calculation you want to perform ("What is my return if I sell now?"), pro-

vide the numbers the site asks for, and get an answer. Quicker and easier than using your calculator—even if you did have all the formulas at your fingertips.

>>**Investorama** (**www.investorama.com**). This site has links to nearly 12,000 financial Web pages, organized by 149 categories so you can easily find what you're looking for. You'll also see a library of articles laden with sensible advice. Investorama is a good source of information about investment clubs. Douglas Gerlach, author of *The Complete Idiot's Guide to Online Investing* (Que Corporation, 1999, $16.99), started the site and writes much of it.

>>**Morningstar** (**www.morningstar.com**). The well-known rating company carries its mutual fund expertise to the Web, where it offers news stories and analysis on the world of funds. There's free access to much of the site, although subscribers ($9.95) get enhanced features.

>>**MSN Moneycentral** (**www.moneycentral.com**). This is Microsoft's entry into the financial Web page business; it features not only a library of personal finance articles but also several interactive tools for investors.

>>**Raging Bull** (**www.ragingbull.com**). This site, which was started by a group of undergrads from Rutgers University and the University of Virginia, is well known for stock chats and bulletin boards. One unique feature is the ability of a reader to choose to ignore annoying posts from a specific screen name. Reading through intelligent posts concerning a stock you're watching can indeed yield insights.

>>TheStreet.com (www.thestreet.com). With its news, information, and stock market commentary, this site is for the active trader. TheStreet.com was begun as a subscription site, but is in the process of transforming into two sites, one free and the other a premium site, RealMoney.com. The premium site will charge $200 a year for earlier access to columnists, real-time stock quotes, and hedge fund manager James J. Cramer's Trading Diary. TheStreet.com will continue to offer its extremely readable columnists, news, analyses of companies, and personal finance information for free.

>>Wall Street Journal (www.wsj.com). The *Journal* is the gold standard for financial news, and this site makes good use of the institution's resources. It carries the newspaper's daily copy but also updates the news during the day. Subscribers can search and read stories that have appeared in the past thirty days for free. A valuable although expensive tool is the ability to search all major business publications for stories on a topic; the search is free, but reading articles costs $2.95 each. This site charges a subscription fee of $59.95 a year, or $29.95 for those who also get the print edition.

>>WallStreetLinks (www.wallstreetlinks.com). This site provides an assortment of Web links, organized neatly by categories. If you're having trouble finding information on a certain subject, try this site.

>>Yahoo Finance (finance.yahoo.com). In conversations with young investors this site always comes up as a favorite. It's the 800-pound gorilla of Internet finance portals: with thousands of message boards, news, and customizable portfolio trackers, it's the first stop for many Internet-vestors.

STOCK MARKET GAMES AND SIMULATIONS

OTHER SITES MENTIONED IN THIS CHAPTER MAY ALSO HAVE stock market games, but the sites below concentrate on this specialty. (See Chapter 9 for more information about stock market games.)

>>**CNBC Student Stock Tournament** (**www.sst.cnbc.com**). Along with information on the tournament (rules, current standings, popular portfolio picks), this site has a useful resources area and a stock bulletin board under the "Cafe" section.

>>**Investment Challenge** (**www.ichallenge.net**). This contest's Web site posts information on current contest standings, rules and registration, and, under "Resources," basic investing.

>>**MainXchange** (**www.mainxchange.com**). Home to the popular online investment simulation contest, this site contains basic market info, a resource center with Web links, information on contest rules and prizes, and links to sponsoring companies, such as Donna Karan.

>>**Stock Market Game** (**www.smgww.org**). This is the oldest and best-known stock market simulation game. Since it began in 1977, more than 6 million kids grades four through twelve have played it. This official site has rules, a sample portfolio, information for teachers, and most important, links to the state sites so you can find out how to register.

>>**Virtual Stock Exchange** (**www.virtualstockexchange.com**). This space is first-rate, dishing out more extensive education-

al information than many game sites. The contests aren't exclusively for students, but the game reports a high participation by college kids.

BOOKS

ALTHOUGH THE WEB HAS THE CAPACITY TO PROVIDE EXHAUStive and timely investing information, you can't find everything there. Books and magazines are not only more portable than online resources, but the best ones also contain an abundance of wisdom and elegant writing.

When I first sat down to pull together this section, I found myself citing dozens of books. But then, after some reflection, I decided that what you need isn't a long recommended reading list but a very selective reading list. (As if you didn't have enough homework!) So, in the interest of brevity, I'm limiting my picks to a half-dozen great, all-around beginning investment books. Check the *Street Wise* Web site (**www.streetwise-teen.com**) for a more exhaustive list of recommendations.

Learn to Earn: A Beginner's Guide to the Basics of Investing and Business, by Peter Lynch and John Rothchild (Fireside/Simon & Schuster, 1995, $13).

Lynch is the fabled Fidelity money manager who once managed the Magellan Fund and has made a career for himself out of educating investors. This book is aimed squarely at beginning investors. One of the highlights is Lynch's historical explanations of capitalism and investing.

Making the Most of Your Money, by Jane Bryant Quinn (Simon & Schuster, 1997, $21).

If I were stranded on a desert island and could have one book—it wouldn't be a personal finance book. But if it were, this thick, all-purpose personal finance reference would be it.

Keep it on your bookshelf, and I promise you'll find yourself turning to it for advice several times a year.

The New Money Masters, by John Train (Harper Perennial, 1989, $10.95).

In this follow-up to Train's classic *The Money Masters,* he interviews investment legends on their strategies and techniques.

The Only Investment Guide You'll Ever Need, by Andrew Tobias (Harcourt Brace, 1998 revised edition, $13).

Tobias is funny and smart. What else do you need? It's easy to confuse this book with another by Tobias, *The Only Other Investment Guide You'll Ever Need* (Bantam, 1989, $9.95), which is also superbly done but deals with slightly less basic investing topics. One word of warning: check to make sure you're reading the most up-to-date revision of this book, which was originally published in 1978. The world of investment changes, even for the classics.

Personal Finance for Dummies, by Eric Tyson (IDG Books Worldwide, 1994, $15.99).

This is another highly readable general guide. Its strength is in its specific recommendations for action.

The Wall Street Journal Guide to Understanding Money & Markets, by Richard Saul Wurman, Alan Siegel, and Kenneth M. Morris (Access Press and Siegel & Gale, 1989, $12.95), and The Wall Street Journal Guide to Understanding Personal Finance, by Kenneth M. Morris and Alan Siegel (Lightbulb Press, 1992, $13.95).

The highlight of these books is the compelling way in which they combine graphics and text to explain investing.

NEWSPAPERS AND MAGAZINES

"WHAT DID YOU READ WHEN YOU WERE JUST LEARNING ABOUT investing?" I once asked a money manager. I was anxious to find the key to the breadth of his knowledge. *"The Wall Street Journal,"* he said apologetically. He was sorry he didn't have a more quotable or exotic answer. He needn't have been sorry; he underscored the must-read reputation the *Journal* has in the investment community. But there are other publications that can be equally enlightening. It's worth getting acquainted with the following publications to see which ones you're most comfortable with. The Internet can beat them hands down on breaking news, but magazines like the ones below can provide perspective and a depth of research that many Web sites just aren't equipped to offer. The leading personal finance magazines are listed in "Personal Finance Magazines Worth Your Time," on page 198.

ORGANIZATIONS
AND ASSOCIATIONS

>>The National Association of Investors Corp. (NAIC) has a youth membership that I discussed in Chapter 8. That membership is a wonderful introduction to an organization that is dedicated to teaching investment basics to ordinary investors. Basic youth membership is $20; deluxe membership is $45.

NAIC
711 W. Thirteen Mile Rd.
Madison Heights, MI 48071
248-583-6242
www.better-investing.org

>>The American Association of Individual Investors (AAII) is a nonprofit investor education group. Among the benefits of

Personal Finance Magazines Worth Your Time

Bloomberg Personal Finance (monthly, 888-432-5820)	**www.bloomberg.com**
Business Week (weekly, 800-635-1200)	**www.businessweek.com**
Forbes (biweekly, 800-888-9896)	**www.forbes.com**
Fortune (biweekly, 800-621-8000)	**www.fortune.com**
Individual Investor (monthly, 888-616-7677)	**www.individualinvestor.com**
Kiplinger's (monthly, 800-544-0155)	**www.kiplinger.com**
Money (monthly, 800-633-9970)	**pathfinder.com/money**
SmartMoney (monthly, 800-444-4204)	**www.smartmoney.com**
Worth (monthly, 800-777-1851)	**www.worth.com**

membership: the *AAII Journal,* which comes out ten times a year, the AAII's local chapters, which sponsor seminars and talks by experts, and yearly publications on mutual funds and taxes, as well as the stock screening program the association sells.

The AAII doesn't have a special membership for young investors; adult membership is $49 a year.

AAII
625 North Michigan Ave.
Chicago, IL 60611
800-428-2244
www.aaii.com

"If a graduating MBA were to ask me, 'How do I get rich in a hurry?' I would not respond with a quotation from Ben Franklin or Horatio Alger, but would, instead, hold my nose with one hand and point with the other toward Wall Street."

WARREN BUFFETT

11

Making a Living
on Wall Street

IF YOU'RE FASCINATED BY THE STOCK MARKET, YOU should consider a career in the investment industry. The smartest career choices always involve finding a way to make a living doing something you already love to do. The securities business, unlike some of the hobbies or interests you may have, does offer a variety of careers to choose from, including brokerage, trading, investment banking, and money management. Try finding a way to make a living out of your video game expertise or your talent for collecting baseball cards!

Working on Wall Street—and we're using that term broadly, since there are lots of jobs in the industry outside of Manhattan—offers some of the same rewards and excitement that investing itself provides. Like investing, jobs in the business can be fast-moving, challenging, and competitive. Another major attraction is that careers in the investment business can be

Average Starting Salaries

THE NATIONAL ASSOCIATION OF COLLEGES and Employers polls 350 college and university career-services offices each year to get data on full-time starting salaries in several fields. Below are what newly minted college graduates were pulling down as starting salaries in fields you might be interested in. These figures are national averages and don't include any annual bonuses, which in some jobs can be a significant amount. These data were reported in September 1999.

Investment banking/corporate finance	$37,130
Portfolio management/brokerage	$33,414
Financial analysis	$36,131
Commercial banking, consumer functions	$29,499
Commercial banking, lending functions	$32,657

SOURCE: SEPTEMBER 1999 *Salary Survey,* NACE. REPRINTED WITH PERMISSION.

highly paid. If you work your way to the top of a major investment firm, you can expect to make millions. Even at lower levels, positions tend to be well paid for the level of experience required. Last year the average student graduating from University of Pennsylvania's Wharton Business School with a bachelor's degree made $41,776 (the salaries ranged from $20,000 to $80,000); the estimated average annual bonus, for recently graduated employees who were eligible for bonuses, was $16,000. In the realm of starting salaries for four-year college grads, that's pretty respectable.

However, the folks who work in these jobs will tell you that they toil long and hard and under intense pressure. The hours can be very unpredictable, especially in the early years of your career.

Opportunities in the securities industry are expected to grow more than jobs in most industries in the near future, because of the rise in personal wealth in this country. Quite simply, as more people have more money to invest, jobs are created in the investment business to help them park it in the right place. Even the financial jobs that aren't strictly tied to individual investing, such as investment banking and corporate finance, benefit from the overall growth in U.S. capital markets.

As a whole, jobs in the securities industry tend to follow the same prosperity curve the market itself does. In boom times, everyone is busy, firms are adding workers, and salaries and bonuses are hefty. But if job security will be high on your list of priorities in a career, the investment business may not be for you. When the market turns down, investors back away from the stock market. When that happens, investment firms announce hiring freezes and even layoffs, and annual bonuses shrink for those who keep their jobs. Just as there's a bull-and-bear rhythm to the market, so there is to the Wall Street job market.

WHAT KINDS OF JOBS ARE OUT THERE?

BEING INTERESTED IN BUSINESS AND GOOD WITH NUMBERS will open up lots of opportunities to you. You could go into accounting or banking, for instance, both of which appeal to the same types of people who love the investment business. Below are some of the typical jobs that are identified more closely with the securities business.

>>**Stockbrokers** are, for many Americans, the public face of Wall Street. Retail stockbrokers, the people who deal with individual investors, are known by other titles at most brokerage firms, including account executives, registered reps, and financial consultants. Although their job titles may be different at var-

ious firms, their job descriptions are similar. Brokers are an investor's agent for buying or selling stocks or other financial products, such as mutual funds or annuities. Being a broker is primarily a sales job. When you start out, you must build up a base of clients. Your firm wants to see you generate a certain level of trading business (which produces commissions for the firm and for you) and expects you to champion the products and stocks it sells. Although trainee brokers may receive a salary, experienced brokers rely on commissions to produce most, if not all, of their paycheck.

In addition to retail brokers, there are also institutional brokers, who act as buying and selling agents for large institutional clients, like corporate pension funds or insurance companies. They may deal only with specific financial instruments (bond brokers only sell bonds, for instance).

STREET SLANG<

GO LONG

Trader talk for **buying a stock,** as in, "I'm long Intel." Think of it as the opposite of shorting.

An undergraduate degree is required for these jobs, and most firms put new hires through an extensive training course that culminates in the new broker taking certain exams that are required before he or she can be licensed to do business. While many brokers acquire a masters in business (MBA) degree or another graduate degree, it's not universally expected, as it is in some other Wall Street jobs. Broker positions tend to have a lot of turnover, as it can be difficult to build up enough of a client base to make a go of the job. For the ones who do make it, it can be a lucrative way to make a living. The average retail broker makes more than $100,000 and the average institutional broker makes more than $300,000, according to the Securities Industry Association.

What does the future hold for this job? The landscape has changed for retail brokers. Once, almost all individual investors used a retail broker, but over the past twenty years, an increasing percentage of investors prefer to pick stocks themselves and trade through discount brokers (which are basically telephone-order takers) or online. It's fair to assume that the brokers who will prosper in the future will need to offer services or top-quality advice that investors can't get through an online site.

>>**Securities analysts** are the stock pickers of the industry. If what you love about investing is researching companies or the economy and trying to figure out which firms and stocks will prosper, then perhaps what you want is a career as an analyst. Analysts may cover a particular industry, such as telecommunications, apparel, or retailing, for a brokerage firm and generate stock picks that are used by brokers as recommendations for their customers. Another analyst career track involves working for large institutional investors, helping them to choose which stocks to invest in. ("Sell-side" analysts work for securities firms—the Merrill Lynches and Smith Barneys of the world—while "buy-side" analysts work for investment management firms, which manage money for mutual funds, large corporate or individual investors, pension funds, or other institutional investors.) In the course of their work, analysts have to read and analyze a company's financial statements, perhaps meet and speak with a company's management, and write reports or make presentations. An undergraduate degree is required and an MBA is generally expected—if not immediately upon hiring, then a few years down the road. In addition, becoming certified as a chartered financial analyst (CFA) is a virtual requirement for analysts a few years into their careers; getting certified requires passing a series of difficult exams. Salaries vary, and for the superstar analysts, the ones whose predictions move stock prices and who are constantly cited in surveys of the best securities analysts, pay can reach into the millions of dollars. Starting salaries for analysts on Wall Street are around $40,000, and an experienced analyst can expect a six-figure salary. Analysts are

Web Sites for Wall Street Wanna-bes

THE INTERNET IS AN INFO-RICH SOURCE for students looking for jobs and internships. Check out the following sites for
general advice and leads on jobs.

www.wetfeet.com
campus.monster.com
www.careerpath.com
www.financejobs.com
www.internships.com
www.internshipprograms.com
www.jobWeb.com
www.rsinternships.com
www.vault.com
www.bloomberg.com/careers

generally eligible for bonuses, which, depending on individual
performance and how good a year it has been for the firm, can
range anywhere from a small percentage of salary to 100 percent
of annual salary or more.

Securities analysts can find themselves getting involved in
wooing clients for a firm's investment banking department,
which can increase their compensation. The career path that
portfolio managers or money managers often take is to start
their careers as securities analysts, then at some point switch to
directly making investment decisions themselves.

>>Investment banking is a term that describes several dif-
ferent functions. Investment bankers might be involved in rais-
ing money for client companies, either by selling stock or some
other type of securities or by arranging for private financing

(often investment banking departments are known as the corporate finance department). It can involve helping to arrange mergers and acquisitions or advising clients on overall financial strategy or specific transactions. There is a well-established career path in investment banking: bright young college graduates are hired with the generic title of "analyst" for a couple of years. They are usually rotated through several departments at the investment banking firm, doing support work for the more senior employees. At the end of two years, it's expected that trainees will go to business school for an MBA or perhaps move on to work at a client company. Investment banking generally involves big money for its lucky participants: annual bonuses range from 25 percent to more than 100 percent of salary.

Trading involves doing the actual buying and selling of stocks, bonds, commodities—any of the financial products that can be bought and sold. When you see that a stock is trading at $49, it's because that's the price that the traders last bought and sold it for. But the floors of the various stock or commodities exchanges aren't the only places trading goes on. The big Wall Street firms have their own traders, who trade with their firm's money. In fact, most institutions that manage money have their own traders.

Trading is an intense job that calls for someone who enjoys making high-pressure, split-second decisions and getting rapid feedback. Unlike corporate strategists, traders know very quickly whether or not they made the right decision. For those who are successful, trading can be lucrative; it too is a position that rewards the productive employee with a year-end bonus. Salaries in trading on Wall Street begin at $40,000 to $50,000, while a head trader might earn $100,000. Bonuses, while they vary tremendously depending on the individual, the firm, and how profitable a year they had, might add anywhere from 20 percent to 100 percent or more to that salary.

For a hilarious inside view of what it's like to be a trader—

or salesperson—at a big Wall Street firm, read the book *Liar's Poker,* by Michael Lewis (W. W. Norton, 1989). The book chronicles Lewis's first few years as a trainee and then bond salesperson at Salomon Brothers and is, by all accounts, as on-target today as it was when it first came out.

WHERE ARE THE JOBS?

NEW YORK CITY ISN'T THE ONLY PLACE TO WORK IF YOU YEARN to be in the securities industry, but there's no doubt that it is considered the center of the financial universe. The largest concentration of jobs in the industry is in New York; Manhattan is home not only to the New York Stock Exchange and smaller exchanges, it is also the main base of the largest firms, such as Merrill Lynch, Morgan Stanley Dean Witter, Goldman Sachs, and others. That said, there are top-notch money managers, pension fund managers, and regional brokerage and investment banking firms all over the country. Chicago is the center of commodities trading, and as places such as the Silicon Valley in California have thrived, investment banking has flourished in San Francisco and the West Coast. There are also the international centers of finance, such as London, Frankfurt, Hong Kong, and Tokyo. And most cities have regional offices of general brokerage houses. If you have your heart set on working in the securities business but are opposed to living in or around New York, never fear. There are positions open elsewhere.

STARTING A JOB SEARCH

JOBS IN THE SECURITIES INDUSTRY ARE DESIRABLE: THEY'RE well paid, interesting, and somewhat prestigious, and they don't involve any heavy lifting. So not surprisingly, these are hotly contested jobs in the marketplace. Especially when times are good, the applicants outnumber the openings. How can you best position yourself to snag one of these jobs?

College students who are toying with the idea of going into this as a career should take as many math, economics, and business courses as they can. While it's not absolutely necessary to major in one of these subjects (career services offices report that humanities majors are also hired in the industry), it is necessary to be able to show you can handle numbers. "You can do that through taking math courses or economics courses that require the use of numbers," says Patricia Rose, director of career services for the University of Pennsylvania's Wharton School.

Along with academic training, you will need industry experience, most notably as an intern (see "Making the Most of an Internship," pages 210–211.) Not only will you gain an impressive entry on your résumé, but you'll also make useful contacts.

> STREET SLANG

DELISTING

If going public is the crowning moment of a start-up business, delisting is the opposite. Basically **it's when a company gets kicked off a stock exchange because it no longer meets the listing requirements.** Examples of when delisting happens: when a company goes bankrupt, gets acquired, or the stock price drops below a certain point, such as $1.

Contacts are extremely important in this business. Contacts won't guarantee you a job, but they can help you get an interview with the company you want or make your résumé stand out from the pile. If you don't have contacts that are immediately obvious, stretch your network a little. Do you have any relatives in the business? Do your parents or grandparents use a stockbroker who could smooth your path into a firm? Many college career-placement offices keep listings of alumni at various firms; these alumni might be willing to help you.

Recruiters from the large Wall Street firms will visit the top-ranked colleges and universities to interview job candidates; if

Making the Most of an Internship

"A GENERATION AGO, an internship was a useful enhancement to one's résumé. Now it is an essential stepping stone," says Mark Oldman, cofounder of Vault.com and coauthor of *The Internship Bible* (The Princeton Review/Random House, $25). According to a survey that Vault.com did of the Class of 2000, some 86 percent of all college seniors will have completed at least one internship by graduation. For ambitious teenagers the question is not should you do an internship, but how can you make the most of one? Oldman shared some insights with us about internships.

What's the difference between a summer job and an internship? The idea of an internship is that the job should have some educational component to it. It may be brown bag lunches with company executives or some supervised practical experience, but it should be educational.

Why do companies like having interns? Interns provide a cost-effective way for companies to check out potential employees. Large companies can save $8,000 per candidate by hiring an intern; that's money the company doesn't have to spend to send someone to recruit on campus and then bring students in for interviews.

How can you find an internship? Try surfing Web sites like Vault.com or using books like *The Internship Bible*. You can also use word of mouth; canvass friends and family to find internships that might interest you.

Are internships only for college students? What about high school students? There is certainly a place for high school students doing internships. In this tight labor market, companies are realizing that many high school students have the maturity to perform well in a corporate setting. At Vault.com, we had a high school intern who was here when we were hooking up computers. He knew more than we did about the technology, and in repayment for his work we gave him some stock options.

How can an intern make the best impression on an employer? You need a mix of diplomacy and initiative. You have to realize you're low person on the totem pole and have realistic expectations. You can't expect to be brokering deals and conferring with the chief executive officer. But on the other hand, nobody wants a wet-noodle intern. You have to be self-sustaining enough so they don't have to micromanage you. You should be able to see projects through with a minimum of supervision, and when you're done with your own projects, you need to have the initiative to generate more projects.

How can an intern effectively network during an internship? You have to realize that in addition to being exposed to the industry and the company, you will meet people who could end up giving you powerful recommendations for jobs or graduate school. At every company there are people who are intern-friendly, who maybe were interns themselves, and others who are indifferent. It's important to try to locate the managers who appreciate interns.

How much money should an intern be paid? Most internships do pay, particularly in the finance field. J.P. Morgan paid $575 a week last summer, although that's at the high end. But the money isn't the important thing; if you're looking for money, you might as well get a job digging ditches.

When should you look for an internship? It varies. Some organizations want you to apply in the fall; others may have openings only in the spring. But certainly by December or holiday break you should start sending out letters.

you're at a school that is on the recruiter's schedule, you're ahead of the game. If not, see if you can make inroads with a local or regional firm; a smaller firm can provide you with a wide range of experiences as a beginner and the chance to make a name for yourself. Call the office manager and ask if you can intern there—for free, if necessary. That will allow you to meet and impress staff members who might provide job leads later on.

Another tactic is to try the Internet sites that are listed at the end of this chapter and the Web sites of some of the better-known Wall Street firms, many of which discuss specific employment opportunities. Not sure which Wall Street firms to look into? An easy way to generate names of top firms is to check the tombstone ads in the back of *The Wall Street Journal.* Those are the ads announcing financial transactions, such as mergers and initial public offerings. The top firms are listed on the various tombstone ads as having managed the transaction.

HIGH SCHOOL EXPERIENCES

HIGH SCHOOL STUDENTS ARE IN A PECULIAR POSITION. MOST of the formal Wall Street or securities industry internships and jobs are really designed for college kids, most frequently kids who are going into their senior year. So what can a high school kid do to nurture his or her interest and get a little experience?

"High school students should get as much extracurricular experience as they possibly can," recommends William Banis, director of career services at Northwestern University. "Do as much reality testing as you can. Join Junior Achievement at your school and get experience being a treasurer of a Junior Achievement company or selling things. Try to understand the functions that go on in your Junior Achievement program, and find opportunities to get exposure to those functions. Try on different roles and see what you find satisfying and what is not so satisfying." High school kids might also contact local brokerage or investment offices; even an unpaid menial job at a firm will give you a glimpse of what the business is like and a chance to make some early contacts.

THE ALL-IMPORTANT INTERNSHIP

IT'S TOUGH TO OVERESTIMATE THE IMPORTANCE OF PUTTING some time in as an employee in the industry. Not only do you get a chance to see what the business is like firsthand and decide whether it truly is for you, but you will also acquire a body of knowledge about the industry—even if it is only about standard office operating procedures. When it comes time to hire full-time employees out of college, who do you think stands a better chance of being chosen: someone who has worked in the industry or someone who just says they'd like to?

Fortunately, the internship has a long and hallowed history in this business. At the college level, companies view internships as a way of getting a look at the best and brightest undergraduates and as a way for students to see whether they like a company, too. College internships can also have the advantage of being well paid. Wharton School undergraduate students, most of them entering their senior year, earned an average of $2,256 a month for full-time summer jobs during the summer of 1998 (the average work week was 55.6 hours); while part-timers earned an average of $1,441 a month (working 27.8 hours). But the money is beside the point; the real value is the leg up it gives you in finding a full-time job.

Matt Hooker, a junior finance major at Notre Dame University in South Bend, Indiana, spent eight weeks last summer as an unpaid intern at Merrill Lynch's retail brokerage office in Manhattan's World Financial Center, a job he found through some personal connections. "My dad uses a broker at another

What if You're Having Trouble Finding an Internship?

ONE CREATIVE WAY TO HELP YOURSELF, says author and Vault.com cofounder Mark Oldman, is to create an internship where none exists. His experience is instructive: "When I was an undergraduate at Stanford, I read about a Rutgers law professor who helped countries draft constitutions. It sounded interesting, so I wrote to him. I think he was impressed with my initiative. I was his research assistant that summer, and that fall, in 1990, he was an adviser to Romania, which was drafting a new constitution. He took me along and there I was with him, hanging out with members of Parliament and the Foreign Minister. The point is, in addition to applying to traditional structured internship programs, think of five or six high profile people you admire and write to them letting them know of your interest in being an assistant. Sometimes the experience may be valuable enough for you to work for no pay.

The other thing I would advise is to think about taking off a fall or spring semester from college for an internship. It's far less competitive, and it may actually be a better time to see what goes on inside a company. I applied for a summer internship with the U.S. Supreme Court when I was in school, and didn't get it, but I told them I'd like to be considered for a fall internship, and got it then. Plus the fall was a much better time to be at the Supreme Court."

Merrill office, and he suggested I call this guy," says Hooker. It was his first experience working in the securities industry, and he explains that he was one of three interns who worked as support staff for a group of three brokers and their assistants. "I did whatever the FCs [financial consultants] and their assistants needed us to do," he says. Those tasks included filing, making copies, and doing the legwork necessary to correct "busted" trades (trades where there has been an error in execution—for example, buying a stock instead of selling it). "The FCs also had us do things like organize client lists by asset values [listing clients in order of how much they have invested] and draft a letter to all their clients telling about a new Merrill Lynch program. We answered phones, and arranged for overnight mail when a client needed a check overnight." Hooker felt he learned volumes about the business; he's hoping to spend time on the institutional side next summer to get a sense of what life is like there. His advice for students who are looking for internships: start early. "I started calling in November to find something for the summer, and I interviewed over January break," he says. And be persistent, Hooker counsels: "I called the guy seven times in a two-week time span before I ever spoke with someone."

Students looking for a place to start their internship search should consult *The Internship Bible,* a 650-page directory of student jobs published by the Princeton Review and Random House and written by Mark Oldman and Samer Hamadeh. It details specific internship programs at specific companies, is updated annually in August, and costs $25. Your local public library may have copies available if you don't want to buy the book.

Index

ABOUT BLOOMBERG

BLOOMBERG L.P., founded in 1981, is a global information services, news, and media company. Headquartered in New York, the company has nine sales offices, two data centers, and 80 news bureaus worldwide.

Bloomberg Financial Markets, serving customers in 100 countries around the world, holds a unique position within the financial services industry by providing an unparalleled combination of news, information, and analytic tools in a single package known as the BLOOMBERG PROFESSIONAL™ service. Corporations, banks, money management firms, financial exchanges, insurance companies, and many other entities and organizations rely on Bloomberg as their primary source of information.

BLOOMBERG NEWS℠, founded in 1990, offers worldwide coverage of economies, companies, industries, governments, financial markets, politics, and sports. The news service is the main content provider for Bloomberg's broadcast media, which include BLOOMBERG TELEVISION®—the 24-hour cable and satellite television network available in ten languages worldwide—and BLOOMBERG RADIO™—an international radio network anchored by flagship station BLOOMBERG® RADIO AM 1130 in New York.

In addition to the BLOOMBERG PRESS® line of books, Bloomberg publishes BLOOMBERG® MAGAZINE, BLOOMBERG PERSONAL FINANCE™, and BLOOMBERG® WEALTH MANAGER.

FOR IN-DEPTH MARKET INFORMATION AND NEWS, visit **Bloomberg.com,** which draws proprietary content from the BLOOMBERG PROFESSIONAL™ service and Bloomberg's host of media products to provide high-quality news and information in multiple languages on stocks, bonds, currencies, and commodities, at **www.bloomberg.com.**

ABOUT THE AUTHOR

SUE STEMBER

JANET BAMFORD has specialized in personal finance reporting for over a decade. Formerly with *Forbes* and *American Lawyer,* she was a coauthor of *The Consumer Reports Money Book* and the author of *Smarter Insurance Solutions* (1996, Bloomberg Press). She has written for *Business Week, Investor's Business Daily, SmartMoney, Worth,* and *Family Business* and is currently a senior editor for *Bloomberg Personal Finance* magazine. She lives in Pennington, New Jersey.